THE BATTLE FOR YORK
MARSTON MOOR 1644

THE BATTLE FOR YORK

MARSTON MOOR 1644

JOHN BARRATT

TEMPUS

First published 2002

PUBLISHED IN THE UNITED KINGDOM BY:
Tempus Publishing Ltd
The Mill, Brimscombe Port
Stroud, Gloucestershire GL5 2QG

PUBLISHED IN THE UNITED STATES OF AMERICA BY:
Tempus Publishing Inc.
2 Cumberland Street
Charleston, SC 29401

British Library Cataloguing in Publication Data.
A catalogue record for this book is available from the British Library.

ISBN 0 7524 2335 5

Typesetting and origination by Tempus Publishing.
PRINTED AND BOUND IN GREAT BRITAIN.

COVER ILLUSTRATIONS:
Front cover image: 'The Battle of Marston Moor, 1644' by John Barker.
Back cover images: Figurines of musketeer and pikeman (c.1638) from staircase of Cromwell House, Highgate; 'Cromwell after Marston Moor' by Ernest Crofts.

CONTENTS

CHRONOLOGY

1643

15 September	'Cessation' or truce between King and Irish Confederates.
20 September	First Battle of Newbury.
25 September	Parliament and Scots sign Solemn League and Covenant.
11 October	Parliamentarian victory at Winceby; Newcastle raises siege of Hull.

1644

19 January	Scots Army of the Covenant crosses English border.
25 January	Sir Thomas Fairfax defeats Lord Byron at Nantwich.
5 February	Indecisive action at Corbridge between Northern Royalists and Scots. Prince Rupert assumes command on Welsh border.
29 February	Sir John Meldrum lays siege to Newark.
4 March	Scots take Sunderland.
7–8 March	Indecisive action between northern Royalists and Scots at Humbledon Hill.
21 March	Rupert relieves Newark.
24 March	Indecisive action between Newcastle and Leven at Bolden Hill.
29 March	Parliamentarians under Waller defeat Hopton and Forth at Cheriton.
11 April	John Belasyse defeated at Selby.
16 April	Newcastle enters York.
21–24 April	Leven and Farfax take up positions around York.
25 April	Rupert goes to Oxford to confer with King.
6 May	Earl of Manchester and Army of the Eastern Association storm Lincoln.

16 May	Rupert sets out from Shrewsbury on first stage of Lancashire campaign.
19 May	Parliamentarians occupy Reading.
25 May	Rupert storms Stockport.
26 May	Earl of Essex occupies Abingdon.
28 May	Rupert storms Bolton.
1 June	Essex and Waller close in on Oxford.
3 June	Army of Eastern Association joins siege of York.
6–13 June	King at Worcester.
8 June	Newcastle opens abortive talks with besiegers.
11 June	Rupert takes Liverpool.
14 June	King writes to Rupert ordering him to relieve York and defeat Allies.
15 June	Newcastle breaks off negotiations with besiegers.
16 June	Allied assault on York repulsed.
22 June	Rupert at Preston.
24 June	Rupert at Clitheroe.
26 June	Rupert reaches Skipton.
29 June	King defeats Waller at Cropredy Bridge.
30 June	Rupert reaches Knaresborough.
1 July	York relieved.
2 July	BATTLE OF MARSTON MOOR.
3 July	Newcastle leaves York for Scarborough and exile in Europe.
4 July	Rupert marches out of York towards Richmond. Allies resume siege of York.
9 July	Royalist victory at Marston Moor proclaimed in Oxford.
12 July	King learns of defeat in despatch from Rupert.
16 July	York surrenders.
21 August	Royalist defeat at Ormskirk.
18 September	Byron defeated at Montgomery.
November	Parliamentarians take Liverpool.

1645

2 March	Langdale relieves Pontefract.
14 June	Royalist defeat at Naseby.
25 June	Carlisle surrenders.

20 July	Pontefract surrenders.
25 July	Scarborough surrenders.
15 October	Northern Horse defeated at Sherburn.
22 December	Skipton Castle surrenders.

1646

3 February	Surrender of Chester.

PREFACE

The city of York, for centuries England's 'northern capital', has witnessed more battles in its immediate vicinity than any other English city. Early encounters between the English and Norse invaders climaxed in 1066 with two major engagements: the defeat of the Northumbrians outside the gates of York at Fulford; and King Harold's speedily reversed, costly victory at Stamford Bridge.

During the 600 years which followed, the area around York witnessed bloody encounters between a variety of opponents. English fought Scots, rebels engaged loyalists, and, on a snowy March day in 1461 during the struggle between the rival Houses of York and Lancaster popularly known as the Wars of the Roses, the largest and bloodiest battle ever fought on English soil took place southwest of the city at Towton.

It was virtually inevitable, therefore, that, when in the summer of 1642 civil war erupted between the forces of King and Parliament, York, of key strategic importance to both sides, would once again be in the forefront of the conflict.

The first six months of 1644 witnessed arguably the most critical and decisive phase of the war. Seemingly faced by deadlock after more than a year of bitter fighting, both King and Parliament sought to obtain a decision in their favour by means of outside intervention. Until early July 1644, it hung in the balance whether the King's English troops from Ireland or the invasion by Parliament's new Scottish allies would prevail, firstly in the bitter struggle for northern England, and then in the outcome of the war as a whole.

For it was increasingly apparent to both sides that whoever gained control of the north, with its resources of manpower, ports and links with the Continent, would gain a probably overwhelming advantage. By the early summer, with York under close siege from the allied armies of Parliament and the Scots, King Charles' nephew, Prince Rupert, staked his army and reputation on relieving the Marquis of Newcastle's northern Royalist forces holding the city and defeating the Allies in a decisive battle.

In an eight-day campaign during late June and early July, the prince came within an ace of stunning success. The climax came on 2 July, on the expanse of Marston Moor, six miles west of York, when between 40,000 and 50,000 men clashed in the largest battle of the English Civil Wars. By the end of the day at least one in ten of them were dead, with many more maimed and wounded. The Royalist cause in the north of England lay in ruins, together with Prince Rupert's legend of invincibility. For his victorious opponents, Marston Moor was a giant step on the road to total victory, and for Oliver Cromwell, one of their principal commanders, the battle was a major milestone on his path to greatness.

Although confusion is an inherent part of the story of any battle, Marston Moor is one of the more perplexing engagements for the historian to reconstruct. It was an unexpected encounter, fought partly in conditions of near-darkness, and few if any of its participants had a clear impression of the exact course of events during the three or four hours of that July evening – or of its outcome until long after the fighting ended. The majority of the senior commanders on both sides had little influence on the conduct of the battle once fighting had begun, and, almost uniquely, most of them would end the night as fugitives. Only two of them, the Marquis of Newcastle and Sir Thomas Fairfax, left detailed accounts, and these relate more to their personal experiences than to the battle as a whole. As is frequently the case in battles of the period, relatively few other detailed eyewitness accounts survive.

Given the relative paucity of contemporary accounts, it is not surprising that over the years a number of sharply differing reconstructions have been made of the course of the battle of Marston Moor. Most are worthy of serious consideration. Recent research, however, into the nature, training, organisation and tactics of the armies of the Civil War, when applied to available contemporary sources and the battlefield itself, have made a new examination of the battle, and especially its place in the northern campaign as a whole, timely and worthwhile.

I owe a considerable debt to the researches of many students in the fascinating field of seventeenth-century military history and the Civil Wars, whose work over the last fifteen years or more has done so much to revolutionise our knowledge of this period. They are numerous, and, though I would mention in particular such names as David Blackmore, Dave Cooke, David Evans, Les Prince, Stuart Reid, Keith Roberts and John Tincey, both they and many other scholars, both past and present, have provided me with invaluable help. As ever, however, any omissions and errors are entirely my own. The last word on Marston Moor has not been, and probably never will be, said.

I would like to thank the patient and ever-helpful staff of various libraries, including the University of Liverpool Library, the British Library and the Bodleian Library for their unfailing assistance. At Tempus Publishing, Jonathan Reeve, Joanna Lincoln and the team have been constantly helpful, patient and encouraging.

I dedicate this book to two who are close to me: my wife Helen, whose forbearance and encouragement belie her almost total lack of interest in all things military, and to my little dog, Muffin, whose enthusiastic explorations of the field of Marston Moor happily did not culminate in his suffering the same sad fate as Prince Rupert's 'Boye'.

1

WINTER OF DISCONTENT,
SEPTEMBER 1643–JANUARY 1644

Throughout the early hours of 21 September 1643, weary columns of Royalist troops trudged along the muddy roads heading north out of the town of Newbury towards King Charles I's temporary capital at Oxford. Throughout the previous day, in bitter fighting outside the town, successive Royalist attacks had failed to dislodge the Parliamentarian army under the Earl of Essex, brought to bay when its communications with its base at London had been severed.

But when the Royalists, suffering from an ammunition shortage, were forced to quit the field, the road home was open again to Essex. The tottering Parliamentarian cause had survived its most serious crisis.

For much of 1643 it seemed to many observers that the English Civil War would end in victory for King Charles. From early summer onwards, a string of Royalist victories, at Adwalton Moor, Roundway Down and Bristol, had left the Cavaliers in control of most of the west of England, Wales, much of the Midlands and virtually all of the north apart from Lancashire and the port of Hull. Pushed back towards their heartlands of the Eastern Association of East Anglia, the southeast and London, the Parliamentarians appeared to be at bay.

But in September the Royalist tide faltered with the King's unsuccessful siege of Gloucester, the Northern Royalists' check before Hull, and, above all, after the failure to destroy Essex at Newbury. A quick victory no longer seemed likely for either side, and instead there was a real danger of the war developing into the kind of bloody stalemate which had devastated so much of Europe during the preceding decades. Only outside support seemed likely to tilt the balance in favour of one side or the other.

For the King, apart from the slim chance of intervention in his favour by a European power, the most likely source of aid was represented by the English forces in Ireland. Parliament, however, turned its eyes towards Charles' long-standing opponents, the Presbyterian regime in Scotland, whom the King had failed to subdue in the Bishop's Wars of 1638 and '39.

1. Archibald Campbell, Marquis of Argyle (1598–1661). Known from his squint as 'the glaed-eyed marquis', Argyle was a clever political operator who headed the Covenanting opposition to King Charles I in Scotland. After a long and not always creditable career, he was executed for treason after the Restoration of Charles II.

From the beginning of 1643 the Scots had been offering to mediate in the English conflict, but on terms which would have brought the church in England into line with the religious establishment in Scotland. Unsurprisingly, the King rejected the offer, but this refusal raised the spectre of a Scottish–Parliamentarian alliance. Unwisely, as it turned out, Charles heeded the advice of the Scottish Duke of Hamilton, who claimed that he could contain by political means the advance of the Presbyterian party headed by the Earl of Argyle, and that Scotland would remain neutral.[1] The King ignored the pleas of the Scots Royalist James Graham, Marquis of Montrose, who urged that he and his supporters should stage a military uprising in Scotland before the Covenanting regime could enter the war.

By the time that Charles realised his mistake, it was too late.

On 1 May 1643, John Pym, the enigmatic West Country lawyer who effectively headed the Parliamentarian opposition to the King at Westminster, proposed the start of negotiations for a Scottish alliance. There was a good deal of unease among many of his associates at the prospect of having another Scottish army on English soil so soon after the troops who had occupied parts of the north of England at the close of the Second Bishop's War had gone home, and talks were slow in starting. The swelling tide of military defeat caused a change of heart, even among the least enthusiastic, however, whilst in Scotland Argyle's influence, and reports of the King's plans to reach an accommodation with the rebels in Ireland spurred the Convention of Estates (the effective 'parliament' of Scotland) into action. Summoned to meet on 22 June, the Estates were given details of Royalist plans to employ Catholic Irish and Highlanders against the Presbyterian government in Scotland, and this threat pushed opinion in favour of an alliance with the English Parliament.

Events now moved rapidly. With alarm among the King's opponents in both England and Scotland heightened by his moves to reach a truce or 'cessation' with the Irish Confederates, on 19 July Parliament agreed to send commissioners, headed by Sir Henry Vane the Younger, a skilled political negotiator, to Edinburgh to settle the details of an alliance. The main obstacle to agreement was the religious question: 'The English were for a civil league, we for a religious covenant', wrote one of the Scottish Commissioners.[2] But expediency to some extent overcame religious principals, and the Scots comforted themselves with the thought that events would prove the 'rightness' of their particular brand of Christianity. It was agreed that the eventual religious settlement of the Three Kingdoms of England, Scotland and Ireland would be decided according to the 'Word of God'.

It was a fudged compromise ripe with the seeds of future dissension, but for the moment military matters were more pressing, and within ten days the outline of the alliance known as 'the Solemn League and Covenant' – 'a treaty born of necessity and nourished by illusory hopes'[3] – were agreed. Robert Baillie, a Scots Commissioner, pondered apprehensively: 'The play is begun, the Good Lord give it a happy end.'[4]

On 17 August the treaty was ratified by the Scottish Estates, and the Scots, dubious about the willingness of Parliament to meet its pledges, informed the English Commissioners that they expected a monthly payment of £31,000 (£100,000 of it in advance) for the maintenance of the army which they now began to raise.[5] Their deteriorating military position left the English Parliamentarians no option but to ratify the Covenant with only minor amendments on 25 September.

The Scots had already begun military preparations when on 28 July the Estates ordered the mustering of a small force which on 18 August secured the undefended English border town of Berwick-on-Tweed without opposition, and full mobilisation followed. Command of the Scots army was given to Alexander Leslie, Earl of Leven, a 63-year-old professional soldier of vast experience who had served for over thirty years in the Low Countries and with the great Gustavus Adolphus of Sweden, before returning home to lead the Scottish forces in the Bishop's Wars. Despite a poor education and sometimes being accused of over-caution, Leven was a canny, methodical soldier and a highly capable general. In Scotland his military abilities were held in high regard.

'Such was the wisdom and authoritie of that old little, crooked souldier', wrote Robert Bailie,[6] 'that all, with ane incredible submission, from the beginning to the end, gave themselves to be guided by him, as if he had been Great Solyman.'

2. John Pym (1584–1643), leader of the Parliamentary opposition to Charles I,
and architect of Parliament's alliance with the Scots.

The Bishop's Wars had given the Scottish authorities useful experience of raising large numbers of troops at short notice. Although the majority of the population had little actual combat experience, there were a large number of Scottish mercenaries who had served in the Continental wars available both to train recruits and to provide useful officer material. During and since the Bishops Wars a great quantity of arms and military equipment had been imported from the Low Countries.

The mobilisation of the Scottish army was based upon the liability for military service of all males between the ages of sixteen and sixty. They were required to provide themselves with stipulated arms and equipment, and appear as required at local musters or 'wapinschaws', where they were inspected and rolls compiled of those judged fit to bear arms.

The Committee of Estates used these rolls as the basis for deciding the numbers of troops to be provided by the shires. Each shire had its own committee responsible for fixing the quota for every burgh and parish within its boundaries, and the actual raising of the required men was carried out by local councils, gentry and ministers. In 1643, orders were given for every fourth and eighth man on the rolls to be levied.[7]

The quotas for each shire were fixed on 1 September, and the actual enlistments took place at a series of musters held 4–20 October.[8] By these means it was planned to raise a total of 26,000 men, organised into twenty-one regiments of infantry, nine cavalry and one of dragoons, which, under the title of the 'Army of the Solemn League and Covenant', were to muster near Berwick on 29 December ready for the invasion of England.

In the interim much would depend on the success of the King's plans in Ireland. Here a major rebellion had broken out in 1641, and in the region of 40,000 troops, raised in Ireland, England, Wales and Scotland, were still engaged, generally with little success, in attempts to defeat the Confederates, as the rebels called themselves. As early as January 1643, King Charles authorised his Lord Deputy in Ireland, James Butler, Earl of Ormonde, to begin negotiations to reach a 'cessation', or truce for one year with the Confederates, and 'bring over the English army to Chester' as soon as terms were agreed.[9]

Ormonde was faced with a difficult task, made no easier by the opposition of significant numbers of his Council and the settlers of English origin, whilst continuing military success made the Confederates raise their own demands. On 15 September, however, agreement was reached, leaving only the areas around Dublin and Cork and various isolated garrisons in English hands. The Scots army in Ulster was left to fend for itself.

The Confederates hoped that a permanent political settlement, advantageous to themselves, would follow, but King Charles had more short-term objectives. It was for the moment sufficient for him that the Cessation released the bulk of the English troops serving in Ireland to be brought home to fight for the Royalist cause. In theory there were probably between 20,000 and 30,000 of them altogether,[10] a mixture of veterans of the 'Old Army' in Ireland, and English and Welsh-raised units sent there since 1641. Since the start of the war a number of individual officers had already come over to fight in England. Most served the King, though a few enlisted with Parliament.

Some estimates of the number of troops who eventually crossed the Irish Sea in order to serve King Charles have been considerably inflated;[11] the most likely total of arrivals by the end of 1644, after which crossings practically ceased, were 6,000 to 11,000 to England, and 2,000 reaching Scotland.[12]

The initial problem facing Ormonde and the Royalist leadership was how to transport the troops across waters dominated by the Parliamentarian navy. Fortunately most of the ships of the 'Irish Guard', based on Milford Haven and southern English ports, were diverted during the critical time by Cavalier successes in the south and southwest. A shortage of suitable Royalist transport was alleviated to some extent by ships captured at the fall of Bristol.

The first troops to reach England came from Munster, and landed in the southwest, where they were added to the army which Ralph Lord Hopton was raising to advance into southeast England. Hopton described them as:[13]

...bold, hardy men, and excellently well officer'd, but the common men were mutinous and shrewdly infected with the rebellious humour of England, being brought over merely by the vertue and loyalty of their officers, and large promises [of pay arrears] which there was then but smale meanes to perform.

After an initial mutiny was firmly suppressed, they performed creditably.

However, Royalist hopes rested mainly on the troops from Leinster (the area around Dublin). These were under Ormonde's direct control, and faced a shorter sea crossing from Dublin to Chester and North Wales, against weaker naval opposition from Parliamentarian armed merchantmen based on Liverpool, than did the forces crossing to the southwestern ports from Munster. These relatively favourable conditions allowed 5,000 to 6,000 troops to be shipped over between November 1643 and February 1644, although shortage of transport meant that they had to be carried in several waves, lessening their intended impact.[14]

Unlike the smaller units which had landed in the southwest, it was planned to use the troops from Leinster in a unified force employing a long-term coherent strategy. The eventual aim was to use them to counter the Scots invasion. On 21 November, Ormonde's agent in Oxford, Arthur Trevor, wrote to the earl:[15]

The expectation of English-Irish ayde is the dayly prayers, and almost the dayly bread of them that love the Kinge and his businesse, and is putt into the dispensary and medicine booke of state as a cure for the Scots.

Several alternative proposals were put forward for employing the troops from Ireland. One, particularly favoured by the King's defeated local commander, James Stanley, Earl of Derby, was to use them to re-establish Royalist control of Lancashire and Cheshire.[16] This achieved, the army could then in the spring march either to reinforce the King in the south or support the Earl of Newcastle against the Scots, whichever seemed most appropriate at the time.[17] In the end, circumstances dictated that the immediate decision be left to the commander on the spot, originally intended to be Ormonde himself, although political considerations eventually prevented him from leaving Dublin.

It had been hoped that Ormonde's presence would ensure the loyalty of his troops, for their reliability was a source of great concern to the Royalist high command. The King's secretary of state, Lord George Digby, voiced their nightmare scenario:[18]

If the armye that is transporting hither, considered as fatall to the rebels here, in case it come over and continue with hearty and entire affections, but fully as fatall to his Majestic's affaires in case it should revolt.

Ormonde hoped he had secured the loyalty of his officers by weeding some out and making the remainder swear oaths of allegiance to the King, but was concerned about the reliability of the rank and file. He expected Parliamentarian agents to

3. A soldier from Ireland (from an illustration of 1647). English soldiers serving in Ireland at this time were notoriously badly supplied and equipped. This figure, with only a shirt, and a knapsack to hold his few possessions, is probably only slightly worse turned out than the troops sent over by Ormonde in 1643.

attempt to suborn them with promises of their arrears of pay, and warned the authorities in Chester, tasked with the reception of the 'Irish' forces, that the troops,[19] 'would be apt to fall into disorders, and will think themselves delivered from prison, when they come to English ground, and they will make use of their libertie to go whither they will.'

New clothing, with pay and provisions, would have to be waiting for the arrivals, as well as a force of reliable troops to keep them 'in awe'. In the previous July the neglected soldiers had been described as 'being now so bare even to rags as doth much dishearten them'.[20]

The urgent need for the Leinster troops was underlined in late October when Cheshire and North Wales Parliamentarian forces under Sir William Brereton and Sir Thomas Myddleton launched a sudden offensive over the Dee into northeast Wales, aimed at forestalling the reinforcements from Ireland. Royalist resistance collapsed, and Chester itself was left dangerously isolated.

Fortunately for the Cavaliers, the first contingent of Ormonde's men, 1,850 foot under Sir Michael Earnley, sailed from Dublin on 16 November, and safely disembarked at Mostyn in Flintshire five days later.[21] Brereton failed to persuade any significant numbers to defect, and had to beat a hasty retreat back over the Dee into

4. John, 1st Lord Byron (c.1600–1652). A member of a strongly Royalist family,
Byron had fought in the Low Countries and the First Scots War. His regiment of horse was
the earliest to be completed for the Royalist army. Byron proved a capable cavalry
commander at Edgehill, Burford, Roundway Down and First Newbury, though his record
in higher command was more mixed.

Cheshire, leaving his isolated garrison at Hawarden Castle to be reduced by the new arrivals.

On the same day (21 November) that Earnley landed, John, Lord Byron, with 1,000 horse and 300 foot, set out from Oxford to take command of the Irish-Royalist forces. Byron, with the approval of Prince Rupert, had been appointed 'Field-Marshal-General' of Lancashire and 'those parts' on 6 November.[22] He was intended to deputise pending the arrival of Ormonde, but circumstances would thrust him into a more prominent role.[23]

Byron was to play a major, and controversial, part in the Marston Moor campaign, and then and subsequently has been the subject of a great deal of criticism. An experienced soldier in his mid-forties, Byron was a member of a strongly Royalist Nottinghamshire family (six of his brothers and an uncle also served in the King's armies), and had gained a fine reputation as a cavalry commander, playing a leading role at Edgehill and Roundway Down, and distinguishing himself in the bitter fighting at Newbury. An ambitious and self-confident man, Byron was eager to prove his mettle in independent command.

On 6 December the second contingent of Leinster troops, 1,250 foot and 140 dragoons, landed at Neston in Wirral.[24] With the surrender of Hawarden Castle two days earlier, northeast Wales was clear of the enemy, and the combined 'Irish' force assembled at Chester. The citizens of that town were not greatly impressed by their arrival, seeing them:[25] 'in very evil equipage... and looked as if they had been used to hardship, not having either money, hose or shoes... faint weary and out of clothing.'

Some of the newcomers' more urgent needs were eased by collections of surplus clothing made among the townspeople, and also an organised manufacture of items throughout northeast Wales. Such sympathy as the plight of the soldiers might have aroused, however, was quickly dampened by their alleged behaviour. Some of them promptly sold the clothing they had been given in order to obtain money for drink, and there were widespread complaints of their drunkenness, swearing, brawling, thieving and refusal to attend church on the Sabbath![26]

Within a few days, disillusionment had become so great that the Chester Assembly offered the Royalist commanders what was in effect a bribe of £100 of the city plate to remove their by now unwelcome guests as quickly as possible.[27]

Byron was in any case anxious to take the field, despite increasingly adverse winter conditions. His aim was to clear Parliamentarian-controlled Cheshire, particularly to capture the enemy headquarters at Nantwich, and then move on into Lancashire. On 12 December, at the head of 4,000 foot and 1,000 horse, he set out from Chester on the first stage of his campaign.

The Royalists gained their first success next day, when a party of firelocks under the redoubtable Capt. Thomas Sanford surprised the enemy-held strongpoint of Beeston Castle in a daring operation which apparently involved scaling the nearly sheer northern face of Beeston Crag under cover of darkness.[28] The Royalist forces spread out across the Cheshire countryside in a ruthless operation which seemed to confirm much of the Parliamentarian propaganda regarding the brutality of the troops from Ireland. The most notorious incident occurred on 26 December, when some armed civilians were smoked out of Bartholmley Church, and shot, allegedly after surrendering. Whilst responsibility seems to have rested with local Royalist troops rather than the soldiers from Ireland, a letter claimed to have been written by Byron and published in a Parliamentarian newsletter, saying that 'I put them all to the sword... for mercy to them is cruelty', gave further fuel to enemy propaganda.[29]

For the moment, however, the tide of events continued to favour Byron. On the same day as the Bartholmley 'Massacre', the Irish-Royalist army engaged the Cheshire Parliamentarians under Sir William Brereton at Middlewich. Brereton had been awaiting reinforcements from Lancashire, but was brought to battle before they arrived, and in a hard-fought action with Royalist troops spearheaded by the regiment commanded by Lord Byron's brother Robert, suffered a

5. Beeston Castle, Cheshire. This strategically important stronghold dominated the West Cheshire Plain and the approaches to Chester. Its situation made it difficult to assault, and Beeston fell to the Royalists on 12 December 1643 in a surprise night attack. The castle was eventually starved into surrender by Parliamentarian besiegers in December 1645.

serious reverse and was forced to retreat across the River Mersey to the refuge of Manchester.[30]

With no enemy left to oppose them in the field, Byron's men closed in on the Cheshire Parliamentarian headquarters of Nantwich, held by a garrison of about 1,500 soldiers and townspeople under Sir George Booth. Since the outbreak of war Nantwich had been fairly well fortified with earthen walls and strong points, or 'mounts', and, once his initial summons to surrender was rejected, Byron was faced with the difficult task of mounting a siege in the depths of winter. He was short both of heavy siege guns and probably of gunpowder, after the capture of an ammunition convoy on its way to him, and, with bitter cold and snow affecting even his hardened veterans, attempted to bring matters to a quick conclusion by launching a general assault on Nantwich on 17 January 1644.

After fierce fighting, in which the women of Nantwich joined their menfolk on the barricades, the Royalists were thrown back with the loss of some 300 men. But despite this reverse, Byron remained justifiably confident of success within a short time. Nantwich was totally isolated, and its defenders believed to be running short of supplies. Unless relief arrived quickly, the town must fall.[31]

6. Sir Thomas Fairfax (1612–71). The eldest son of Ferdinando, Lord Fairfax, Sir Thomas served as his father's second-in-command with the Northern Parliamentarian forces in 1642–43. A charismatic commander in battle, Fairfax had a tendency to rashness which sometimes led to his undoing. He won a notable victory at Wakefield (21 May 1643) and played a major role in the Parliamentarian success at Winceby (15 October 1643).

At Westminster, the Parliamentarian leadership were keenly aware of the crisis in Cheshire. Their problem lay in finding troops to mount a relief operation. The choice fell on Sir Thomas Fairfax and his 1,800 horse and dragoons who were wintering in Lincolnshire, mainly because these were the only troops immediately available.

Sir Thomas Fairfax is another of the key figures in the story of the Marston Moor campaign. Aged thirty-two, Fairfax, with limited experience of war on the Continent, had served since the start of the war as second-in-command to his father, Ferdinando, Lord Fairfax, in the Yorkshire Parliamentarian forces. A fiery leader in battle, when his normally diffident personality was transformed, 'Black Tom' had won a number of notable successes, notably at Wakefield (21 May 1643) and with Cromwell at Winceby in October. He had, however, a tendency to rashness which on occasion caused him serious difficulties.

Fairfax was unenthusiastic about his new task:[32] 'I was the most unfit of all their forces, being the worst paid, my men sickly and almost naked, for want of clothes.'

Higher authority proving adamant, however, Fairfax remedied such deficiencies as he could from his own pocket, and set off through the Midlands, en route to Manchester, picking up a few reinforcements as he went. Byron was aware of Fairfax's movements, which may have been an additional reason for his attempted assault on Nantwich on 17 January. Three days earlier, Byron's cavalry, with 1,000 picked foot, had surprised Fairfax in his quarters at Newcastle-under-Lyme, and inflicted a severe mauling on him.[33]

It may be that Byron thought his opponent more badly damaged than was in fact the case, for Sir Thomas pushed on to Manchester, where he met with a luke-warm welcome from the Lancashire Parliamentarian leadership, more concerned about the threat from Newcastle's forces across the Pennines than the fate of Nantwich. Fortunately some of the 'inferior officers and common soldiers' proved more co-operative, and within a few days Fairfax was able to muster a force consisting of his own men and some Lancashire and Cheshire troops totalling in all about 1,800 horse and dragoons and between 2,500 and 3,000 foot. On 21 January, not without considerable misgivings, Sir Thomas set out through the deep snow, bound for the relief of Nantwich.[34]

Fairfax had few illusions about the difficulties he faced, for he knew that Byron's 'Irish' were:[35]

> Men of great experience who had run through all sorts of services, and were not new to the Policies of Warre... acquainted with the greatest hardship, habituated to cold and want, and whatever suffereing a winter siege could require... They were put in heart by their former successes, and that would make them the more desperate, and they were valiant before, being used to nothing but conquests...

Byron would later cite problems which the hostility of the local population had posed for him when trying to obtain intelligence of enemy movements, and it is unclear how quickly he became aware of Fairfax's march. However he was certainly

7. The reality of the ragged appearance of the typical seventeenth-century army on campaign is captured in this contemporary painting of the Spanish Army of Flanders.

aware of his approach no later than the afternoon of 24 January, when one of his cavalry patrols clashed with Fairfax's men in Delamere Forest. The Parliamentarians halted for the night on Tilstone Heath, eight miles from Nantwich, knowing that they must fight next day.

Byron evidently hoped to maintain the siege until the last possible moment, planning to give the garrison as little time as possible to replenish their provisions whilst he dealt with Fairfax. He planned to engage him at a safe distance from Nantwich, hoping thus to minimise the danger of intervention by its defenders.

But his strategy, sound enough in itself, was wrecked by a sudden thaw during the night, which caused the swollen River Weaver to sweep away a temporary bridge connecting the besieging forces operating on either bank, and leaving the largest part of the Royalist army isolated on the eastern side of the river, and facing a lengthy march before it could link up with the detachment, under Col. Richard Gibson, stationed on the west bank, nearest to Fairfax.

Gibson, with perhaps 1,000 foot took up position around Acton Church, about 1.5 miles west of Nantwich, anxiously awaiting the arrival of Byron and the remainder of the army.

Meanwhile, brushing aside a small Royalist outpost at Barbridge, four miles from Nantwich, where Byron had probably intended to make his stand, Fairfax approached Acton at about 1 p.m. However, delays in bringing up his guns and baggage had allowed most of the Royalist troops from the east bank of the Weaver to cross and join Gibson.

8. Soldier from Ireland, 1643. The musket rest which this man has was gradually phased out as lighter weapons were introduced. Note the piece of white paper in his hat, acting as an identifying 'field sign' in battle.

Fairfax, admitting that 'we gave him [Byron] time to obtain what he sought for',[36] now decided on a move so rash that it has been likened to 'attempted military suicide'.[37] He would bypass the Royalist position and march northeastwards across the fields in order to link up with the Nantwich garrison. In the process he exposed the right flank of his army, strung out in column with horse at front and rear and headed by pioneers cutting gaps in the hedges, to potentially devastating attack.

Although the Royalists were probably still deploying, and the enclosed nature of the ground made a co-ordinated assault difficult, Fairfax was taking an enormous gamble, and one which brought him close to disaster. At about 3 p.m. Byron launched a general attack, with Gibson, commanding his own, Warren's and Earnley's regiments on his right, attacking the enemy flank and Robert Byron's regiment on the left, swinging in against the rear of Fairfax's column.

The battle, between two armies closely matched in numbers, was hard-fought, and hung in the balance for over an hour. Two incidents eventually decided the outcome. Some of Byron's foot, apparently from Henry Warren's regiment, 'upon an instance unexpected' gave ground. Byron alleged treachery, claiming that at least sixty men suddenly changed sides and opened fire on their own comrades, but this is not mentioned by Parliamentarian sources, and it is equally possible that ammunition shortages were a key factor. As the Royalist attack faltered, the Nantwich garrison made a well-timed sortie, brushed aside the weak force guarding the western exit of the town, and took Gibson's foot in the rear.

Although the Royalist horse, who had played little part in the battle, and the 800 men of Robert Byron's regiment of foot were able to extricate themselves largely intact, the bulk of the remaining 'Irish' foot were lost, with 200 dead and 1,500 taken prisoner. As an independent fighting force, the army from Leinster had ceased to exist, and about a third of the prisoners eventually took service with the Parliamentarians.[38] Some of the others were eventually exchanged in the spring.

Byron had been largely the victim of circumstances beyond his control, but he had suffered a major blow, and Royalist plans were seriously disrupted. The defeated Royalist commander wrote bitterly, and not entirely fairly, to Ormonde that the English troops from Ireland were largely untrustworthy, and asking that 'native' Irish should be sent over in future,[39] 'the English excepting such as are gentlemen not being to be trusted in this war.'

It would be left for Prince Rupert, appointed on 6 January as captain-general of Wales and its Borders, instead of Ormonde, to attempt a salvage operation. In the meantime, bereft of their promised support from the 'Irish' army, the Earl of Newcastle and the Northern Royalists would have to face the Scottish invaders as best they could.

2

THE SCOTS INVASION AND THE SIEGE OF YORK,
JANUARY–JULY 1644

William Cavendish, First Marquis of Newcastle, is one of the most vilified of all the Royalist commanders. The verdict of Sir Philip Warwick, who served for a time on Newcastle's staff, was typical:[1] 'His edge had too much of the razor in it, for he had the tincture of a romantic spirit, and had the misfortune to have something of the poet in him.' This view has been echoed by many modern writers, but is not altogether a fair one.

Aged fifty on the outbreak of war, Newcastle was vastly wealthy, and had great influence in the north of England, particularly Northumberland and Durham, where he had considerable estates. It was this, rather than his virtually non-existent military experience, which led in June 1642 to Newcastle's appointment as the King's general of Northumberland, Durham, Cumberland and Westmoreland. He was tasked with securing a landing place (initially Newcastle-upon-Tyne) for supplies from abroad and eventually for the disembarkation of Queen Henrietta Maria and the munitions and officers she was gathering in Holland.

In July the King greatly extended Newcastle's authority, making him general of all Royalist forces north of the Trent, including Lancashire and Cheshire, as well any troops raised in East Anglia.[2] It was a huge command, which it proved quite impracticable to administer effectively, so that the commanders in the further reaches of Newcastle's empire – the Earl of Derby in Lancashire and Lord Loughborough in the Midlands – were left largely to their own devices.

Early successes gained in Yorkshire by the Parliamentarians under Ferdinando, Lord Fairfax, forced Newcastle reluctantly to commit his forces to stabilise the Royalist position there, and though this was achieved, he was unable to undertake further major operations until the queen and her great munitions convoy had been safely dispatched to Oxford in June 1643. Freed by her departure, Newcastle moved

9. James King, 1st Lord Eythin (1598?–1652). After serving with the Swedes, this Scottish professional soldier in March 1643 became lieutenant-general to the Earl of Newcastle. He served effectively if unremarkably as Newcastle's 'chief of staff' for the remainder of the existence of the Northern Army. It may be that the prospect of fighting his fellow countrymen after the Scots entered the war caused Eythin some unease.

decisively, at the battle of Adwalton Moor (30 June) smashing the hold on the West Riding of Lord Fairfax and his son, Sir Thomas, and forcing them to take refuge in the great fortress port of Hull.

Newcastle had achieved both of the main objectives set him, but ironically his very success helped to hasten the alliance between Parliament and the Scots. Before long, he would face the prospect of war on two fronts.

The Northern Army compared favourably with the other Royalist forces. Newcastle compensated for his own lack of military experience by appointing professional soldiers to key positions. Most significant for events at Marston Moor was his lieutenant general (effectively chief of staff), James King, later Lord Eythin. King, a Scotsman, had served with the Swedes during the Thirty Years War. His fellow countryman Sir James Turner, another experienced soldier, said of King that he was:[3] 'a person of great honour, but what he had saved of it in Germany, where he made a great ship wrack of much of it, he lost in England.'

King was perhaps best known for his role at the Battle of Lemgo in 1638, where his failure to support Prince Rupert was alleged to have led to the latter's capture.

10. William Cavendish, 1st Marquis of Newcastle (1592–1676). Sir Philip Warwick, who served with Newcastle, said of him: 'His edge had too much of the razor in it, for he had a tincture of a romantic spirit, and had the misfortune to have somewhat of the poet in him.' A fine horseman, Newcastle, for reasons now obscure, had been unpopular at Court even before the war. As a general in the north, he carried out a difficult task with a fair degree of success, but was hindered as much by his own sensitive nature as by the enemy.

He seems however, so far as his service with Newcastle prior to Marston Moor is concerned, to have been a generally competent if sometimes overly cautious officer.

Although the northern forces had initially been short of arms, by late 1643 foreign imports, with some local manufacture, probably resulted in their being as well armed as any other forces involved in the war.[4]

After his victory at Adwalton Moor, Newcastle yielded, with some reluctance, to pressure from the King and moved to besiege Hull. As he was probably well aware, he lacked the strength to storm the town, breach its formidable defences or blockade it by sea. The siege was ended by a major Parliamentarian sortie and the defeat of the Lincolnshire Royalists by Oliver Cromwell and Sir Thomas Fairfax at Winceby on 11 October.

It seems clear from the evidence that Newcastle was becoming increasingly exasperated by what he saw as ignorant and malicious criticism and intrigue by enemies at court. Sensitive by nature, he bitterly resented jibes that he was a 'lamentable man, as fit to be a general as a bishop',[5] or, from members of Prince Rupert's circle, that he lay in bed until 11 a.m., combed his hair until noon, and so the work was done.

His concern for his own position, and the threat which he felt it to be under, was highlighted by Sir Phillip Warwick:[6]

> There was nothing he apprehended more than to be joined to the King's army, and to serve under Prince Rupert, for he designated himself to be the man who should turn the scale, and to be a distinct and self-subsisting army, wherever he was.

But after his failure before Hull, Newcastle realised he faced a struggle against increasingly adverse odds. Whilst contending with the imminent Scots invasion, he would also have to protect the southern and western parts of his territory from attack by the Parliamentarians. His resources were plainly inadequate to cope with all of these threats. Newcastle spent the autumn consolidating control of Derbyshire, sending Sir Thomas Glemham north to make what preparations he could for the coming of the Scots. Glemham met with little enthusiasm from the local gentry, and could raise few troops.

January 1644 saw the far north of England hit by the same severe wintry conditions which were hindering the operations of Lord Byron and Sir Thomas Fairfax in Cheshire. It may be that Newcastle and his commanders believed the weather to be too bad for the Scots to take the field, but their hopes were dashed on 18 January, when Leven and his army began crossing the River Tweed.

They declared in a proclamation to have come:[7]

> ...to rescue His Majesty's person and honour so unhappily entangled in the counsels of those whose actions speak their ends to be little better than popery and tyranny.

It was an unconvincing claim. Leven in fact had two major objectives: to secure the town of Newcastle and the mouth of the Tyne, both to safeguard his own communications and to re-open the supply of coal to the citizens of London; and secondly to destroy the northern Royalist army.

The Scots army theoretically totalled 18,000 foot, 3,000 horse and dragoons, and a powerful artillery train. However many regiments, particularly among the foot, were severely under-strength, and figure of 15,000 for the infantry may be closer to actual figures.[8]

Whatever their actual total, the Scots greatly outnumbered the few thousand mostly ill-armed levies which Sir Thomas Glemham had been able to muster, and the Royalist commander took refuge inside the defences of Newcastle-upon-Tyne, sending urgently to the marquis for help.

Newcastle had no option but to divide his forces. Lord John Belasyse, with about 5,000 Yorkshire infantry, about half of Newcastle's total force, and some 1,500 cavalry, was left to try to contain the Parliamentarian threat in the south. Newcastle himself, initially with 5,000 foot and about 2,000 horse, hurried north to meet the Scots, planning to pick up more levies in Durham as he went. Before leaving York, he wrote an impassioned letter to Prince Rupert, vividly describing his plight:[9]

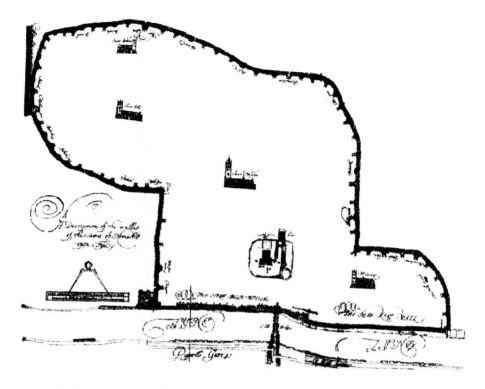

11. The defences of Newcastle-upon-Tyne in 1640. The medieval walls were strengthened by a number of outworks both during the Scots Wars and after 1642.

I know they tell you, sir, that I have great force: truly I cannot march five thousand foot, and the horse not well armed. The Scots advanced as far as Morpeth, and they are fourteen thousand as the report goes. Since I must have no help, I shall do the best I can with these…

It was a close-run race. Fortunately for the Royalists, foul weather, particularly the swollen rivers, slowed the Scots advance, the foot soldiers crossing fords 'up to their middles, and sometimes to the arme-pits.'[10] These conditions, as well the need to wait for his artillery train to catch up, reduced Leven's pace to a crawl. By 2 February he was no further south than Morpeth, allowing Newcastle, with a small cavalry escort, to reach Newcastle-upon-Tyne ahead of him that night.

The town had medieval walls, which had been repaired during the Bishop's Wars and since 1642. Glemham had continued to strengthen them, and had also added a few outworks. Leven's advance guard arrived before Newcastle on 3 February. The town was defended only by Glemham and some Trained Band troops, and the next few hours were critical. The Scots summons to surrender was rejected, and Leven's men stormed an outwork on the northeastern side of Newcastle, forcing the defenders to abandon the suburb of Sandgate. Fortunately, however, the Scots heavy siege guns, being transported by sea to the port of Blyth, had been delayed by the bad weather, and the remainder of Newcastle's forces, reinforced to some extent by troops raised in Durham, now began arriving, frustrating a Scots attempt to push south across the Tyne. This, according to Sir James Turner, a professional soldier with little respect for the Covenanting leadership, was a sadly mismanaged affair in which the Scots commanders, when trying to construct a bridge of boats, forgot the effects of the tide, and ended in the panic-stricken withdrawal of most the troops involved.[11]

During the next fortnight both sides pushed outposts further up the Tyne, the Scots seeking unguarded crossing points, and the Royalists attempting to parry their moves. Newcastle and Eythin sent a pessimistic situation report to King Charles, restating the weakness of their forces, their disappointment that Lord Byron's troops had not been sent to reinforce them, and their shortage of munitions, and pointing out that:[12]

> Sir Thomas Fairfax's success in Cheshire hath made him capable of drawing from Lancashire a great force into the West Riding of Yorkshire, which he is ready to do. My Lord Fairfax hath sent forth of Hull into the East Riding two thousand foot and five hundred horse, all threatening to march towards us, which will make a very great body. And by this your Majesty may perceive where the seat of the war is likely to be...
>
> And now we thought it our duty to represent truly to your Majesty our present Condition, and humbly desire your Majesty's express commands – whether we shall still continue in a defensive posture, and expect some assistance, as well of force as ammunition, from your Majesty, or whether, upon this great equality, so we shall adventure to hazard the loss of this army, and so of all the North, by giving them battle...

The dispersal of the Scottish forces resulting by their movement along the Tyne seemed to offer the Royalists an opportunity to defeat them in detail. A series of counterattacks were planned, but suspicions of treachery, particularly among the many Scottish professional soldiers serving with Newcastle's army, caused most of the operations to be called off. On 19 February, however, a mixed force of horse and foot under Sir Marmaduke Langdale attempted to surprise the quarters of a Scottish cavalry brigade at Corbridge. The plan went awry when the Royalists found the enemy on the alert, and the lord general's and Lord Kirkudbright's Regiments of Horse drawn up to receive them. A confused action with varying success for both sides followed. One of Langdale's officers, Col. Sir Robert Brandling, was captured in single combat by Lt-Col. Elliot of the lord general's regiment. A second Royalist force under Sir Gamelial Dudley successfully beat up Col. Frazer's Dragoons, quartered in Ovingham, before being forced to retire over the Tyne again.

On balance, honours were fairly even, with about sixty dead and 200 prisoners, roughly half coming from each side.[13]

12. Scots cavalry trooper. Most cavalrymen probably only wore their helmets when action was expected. Many of the Royalist Northern Horse were probably similar in appearance.

On 21 February Leven got under way again. Leaving six infantry regiments and a few horse to mask Newcastle-upon-Tyne, he moved his main force four miles upstream to the Corbridge-Ovingham area. In response Langdale, unable to face the full strength of the Scots army, evacuated Hexham, After a brief pause caused by a return of wintry conditions, on 28 February Leven forded the Tyne at three points.

The Scots, according to their own account, got across the Tyne 'in the nick of time', for its level was steadily rising because of melting snow. Reaching the Derwent, they:[14]

> ...found an impetuous flood, and still waxing so, that there was no possibility for our Foot to march over, but at a narrow tree-bridge neer Ebchester; where the half of our Foot marched over the Bridge by files, the other half stayed on the other side till the next day...

Until they reached the relative safety of Sunderland on 4 March, Leven's men were strung out, suffering severely from the bad weather and seemingly vulnerable to a Royalist attack. Newcastle, however had decided against opposing the Scots crossing of the Tyne:[15]

13. Alexander Leslie, 1st Earl of Leven (1588–1661). The illegitimate son of George Leslie, Captain of Blair Atholl Castle, Leslie had a rudimentary education; he would claim later: 'I got the length of the letter "g"!' From about the age of twenty he served with the Dutch and Swedish forces, reaching with the latter the rank of field marshal. He joined the Covenanters in 1640, when he was their lord-general. He was created Earl of Leven by a somewhat unwilling Charles I in the same year.

First after I had made true inquisition of the passes over the River Tyne, I found there was so many fordable places betwixt Newcastle and Hexham, about twelve miles distant one from the other, that it was impossible with my small number of Foot to divide them so as to guard and make good every place, but to hazard the loss of them at any one place, and yet not do the work; so I resolved of two evils to choose the less, and left them to their own wills.

Leven had gained a decided advantage. In Sunderland he had shelter for his troops and a port at which to land supplies, whilst he was also in a position to threaten the Royalist lines of communication. The marquis, leaving the local Trained Bands to hold Newcastle-upon-Tyne, had no option but to pull his main army back southwards. On the same day that Leven entered Sunderland, however, the marquis had been reinforced by Sir Charles Lucas, a capable cavalry commander sent from Oxford to act as Newcastle's lieutenant-general of horse, bringing with him about 2,000 cavalry, mainly from the Midlands, and some hastily raised Durham foot.[16]

Whilst Newcastle was still outnumbered by the Scottish foot, the Royalist horse was now superior in both quality and numbers, and he felt able to act more aggressively. On 6 March he set his army in motion, crossing the River Wear by the new bridge below Lumley Castle and pressing on towards the Scots.

Leven was justifiably cautious about the prospects of a major action. His cavalry, with their mostly smaller, lighter mounts, were generally outclassed by their Royalist counterparts, whilst Sir James Turner said of the Scottish infantry:[17] 'I found the bodies of the men lustie, well-clothed and well money'd, but raw, untrained and undisciplined; their officers for the most part young and inexperienced.'

After some skirmishing, Scots cavalry outposts fell back to their quarters, but some kind of encounter was now inevitable, and the next day (7 March) both armies formed up for battle. The Scots took up a strong position on Humbledon Hill, to the southwest of Sunderland, whilst Newcastle probably deployed on Hastings Hill, to the east of Penshaw Hill. During the morning continuous heavy snowfall prevented any action, but in the afternoon skirmishing developed. It soon became clear, however, that the enclosed nature of the ground and the strength of the Scottish position, protected by a stream, from which they were unwilling to be drawn, made a major engagement impracticable, and at nightfall the Royalists fell back to Penshaw Hill, both armies spending a miserable night in the open.

Next morning Newcastle attempted to force the Scots to give battle by outflanking their position and marching on Sunderland. However the Royalists were hindered by the heavily enclosed nature of the ground, and slowed by parties of Scots musketeers deployed in strong naturally defensible positions. Seeing that the Scots:[18]

> ...stood in their best postures to receive us, having the sea behind them and on the left hand the town [Sunderland], the hill and inaccessible places, by which we must have fetched a great compass about, that they would have been on the same hill again to have received us that way. By this time, the evening caused us to withdraw towards the higher ground, where being saluted with cold blasts and snow, our horses' sufferance with hunger, that we seemed so far to become friends as in providing against those common enemies.

Next day, 9 March, Newcastle withdrew to Durham. During the Royalist retreat the rearguard provided by some of Sir Charles Lucas's horse administered a rough handling to an outpost of Scottish dragoons, claiming to have killed forty and captured twenty of them, including some English deserters.[19] It was a minor tactical success which could not conceal the Royalist failure to bring the enemy to decisive battle. Newcastle was keenly aware that Belasyse in Yorkshire was frighteningly vulnerable to the superior Parliamentarian forces massing against him, whilst Leven had only to keep his own army intact until such time as the English Parliamentarians were able to come to his aid. The marquis warned Prince Rupert:[20]

14. A Scots pikeman. He wears the standard dress of the Scots army, a hodden grey coat and breeches, and a Scots blue bonnet. Like most of his English counterparts by this time, he has no armour.

...the Scots are as big again in foot as I am, and their horse, I doubt not, much better than ours are, so that if your Highness do not please to come hither, and that very soon too, the great game of your uncle's will be endangered if not lost.

The return of winter weather forced both armies back into their quarters. Despite their possession of Sunderland, the Scots supply situation was still serious:[21]

Our army hath been in very great straits for want of victual and provisions. The enemy hath wasted and spoyled all the Countrey, and driven away all Before them. And five Barques sent from Scotland to us, with provisions, are lost... So that sometimes the whole Army hath been ready to starve, having neither Meat nor Drink: we never have above twenty-and-four hours provisions for them.

With his supply ships disrupted by the weather, Leven attempted to clear his landward communications with Scotland, and on 20 March his troops gained a heartening success when they stormed one of the Royalist forts covering the mouth of the Tyne at South Shields. Three days later Sir James Lumsden's infantry brigade, 3,000 strong, left the forces blockading Newcastle-upon-Tyne in order to join the main field army.

For his part, Newcastle still hoped to bring on the decisive battle on which so many of his hopes rested. On 23 March he moved out of Durham along the north bank of the Wear. Next day, according to a Scots account:[22] 'Being the Lord's day, the enemy marched towards our Quarters intending to have set upon us at Sermon time, and being a foggie day to have surprised us.'

However Leven got wind of the Royalist approach, and drew up his own forces on a hill known as Whitburn Lizard. The Royalists took up position about three miles to the southeast, on Bolden Hill. Between them lay an area of flat moor land, bisected by the Don stream, and containing three small villages, West and East Bolden and Cleaden, surrounded by some hedged enclosures.

Both sides pushed musketeers forward to line the hedges on the level ground, and the Scots version of what followed states:[23]

> …the Armies could not join, the field between us being so full of hedges and ditches, our Dragoons beganne the play, and then the Musqueteers in the hedges upon both sides, our bodies of foot advancing at all Quarters to the hedges, the Enemies' Cannon discharging upon them an houre and a halfe with very small hurt: This service continued very hot, till after twelve of the clock at night: Many Officers, who have been old Souldiers, did affirm they had never seen so long and hot service in the night time; there was divers killed on both sides but the number of their slaine did very farre exceed ours, as wee understood by the dead bodies wee found the next day upon their ground, besides the seven Waggons draught of dead, and hurt men not able to walk, that the Constable of Bouden affirmed he saw carried away. The Enemy quit their ground, where they left much of their powder, match and armes behinde them; and retired to the Hill where the Body of the Army lay.

The two sides were probably fairly evenly matched, Newcastle having 5,000–6,000 foot, and the Scots rather more. It seems that about four of Newcastle's foot regiments bore the brunt of the action on the Royalist side. According to the not always reliable Royalist newsletter, *Mercurius Aulicus*:[24]

> The fight began about three in the afternoon and continued from that time till night, and continued more or less till next morning, the rebels all this while being upon their own Mickle Midding, and there they lay all night.

15. Musketeer on campaign. Although clothing was ideally issued once a year,
it quickly deteriorated in the rigours of campaign life. This soldier, who could be either
Royalist or Parliamentarian, has a broad-brimmed felt hat, which,
although not generally standard issue, was commonly worn. Note that the lock
of his musket has been wrapped to protect it from the weather.

During the day, Leven attempted to ship some of his heavy cannon across the Wear
in support of his foot, but two were lost in the river.

Next morning it seemed likely that action would be resumed. The Scots had
pulled their forward troops back to their main position on Whitburn Lizard, and after
eyeing the enemy for most of the morning, Newcastle decided they were too
strongly posted for him to attack. Throwing up field works to protect some light
guns, which were reinforced as a rearguard by cavalry, in the course of the afternoon
the marquis began withdrawing to Durham. Some sharp fighting took place between
opposing horse, until the Scots lancers were checked in a brisk counterattack by Sir
Charles Lucas and his horse.[25]

Losses are unclear; the Royalists admitted to 240 dead 'common soldiers', and
claimed to have killed 1,000 Scots.[26] The true figures for the Scots were probably
similar to those of the Royalists.

Bolden Hill had very nearly been the decisive action which Newcastle sought, but time was fast running out. He seems to have been despondent of success, and at about this time both he and Eythin evidently offered their resignations. Charles implored them to reconsider, pleading with Newcastle, and at the same time apparently confirming some of his darkest suspicions:[27]

> The truth is, if either you or my Lord Eythin leave my service, I am sure all the North is lost... The Scots are not the only, or (it may be said) the least enemies you contend with at this tyme... All courage is not in fighting; constancy to a good cause beeinge the chiefe, and the dispysing of slanderous tongues and pennes being not the least ingredient.

On 1 April Leven advanced again, moving south to Easington, where he could begin to squeeze the Royalist supply lines into Durham. A week later the Scots pushed on westwards to Quarrington Hill, another strong position from where they threatened Royalist communications still further.

In response, Newcastle abandoned Durham on 12 April and headed for Bishop Auckland. He hoped to make a renewed stand along the line of the River Tees, but on the line of march news reached him of long-feared disaster in Yorkshire.

Belasyse had inherited an unenviable situation in his Yorkshire command. According to the Duchess of Newcastle's somewhat tendentious *Life* of her husband, Belasyse had been left:[28] 'sufficient forces for the defence of that country... [and] had strict orders not to encounter the enemy, but to keep himself in a defensive posture.'

If these were in fact the orders given to Belasyse, they were highly unrealistic. Doing the best he could, faced not only by numerically superior forces, but by dissension among local Royalists, Belasyse organised his small force into three commands. One at Leeds was to endeavour to hold the West Riding against imminent attack from across the Pennines by Sir Thomas Fairfax, reinforced by the Lancashire Parliamentarians. Another detachment, based at Malton, was to counter Lord Fairfax's troops operating out of Hull, whilst Belasyse himself with his remaining men formed a reserve at York. Initially he was reinforced by Sir Charles Lucas and his brigade from the Midlands, but early in March these were summoned northwards by Newcastle.

At the same time pressure on Belasyse began to increase. Already in mid-February Parliamentarian horse from Hull had begun a series of successful raids on Royalist quarters in the East Riding, and now Sir Thomas Fairfax detached troops under Col. John Lambert to re-establish a Parliamentarian presence in the West Riding. Lambert occupied Bradford, and on 6 March defeated two weak Royalist cavalry regiments at Hunslet. Establishing his operational headquarters at Selby, a strategically placed crossing point of the River Ouse, Belasyse concentrated virtually his entire force of 1,500 horse and rather less than 5,000 foot. On 25 March he struck at Lambert in Bradford, but after several hours' fierce fighting was forced to fall back when his ammunition ran low.

Selby itself was soon under threat. Sir Thomas Fairfax had been summoned back from Lancashire by his father, and, ignoring orders to march north in support of the Scots, the Fairfaxes decided to strike at Belasyse's little army at Selby. Lord Fairfax had been reinforced by perhaps 2,000 foot from the Midlands under the Scottish professional soldier Sir John Meldrum, bringing the total strength of the combined Parliamentarian army up to about 7,000 men.

Early on 11 April the Parliamentarians launched three simultaneous assaults on Selby. From behind improvised barricades, the Royalists for a time put up a fierce resistance, until, backed by Sir Thomas and his cavalry, Lord Fairfax's own regiment of foot broke into the town. The Royalists rapidly collapsed. Belasyse and the majority of his foot were captured, whilst his cavalry fled to the refuge of York. The entire Royalist position in Yorkshire had been undermined, and the city of York itself was in grave danger.[29]

The Marquis of Newcastle could delay no longer; his attempt to hold back the Scots had to be abandoned in favour of a dash to save the northern capital.

The march south came close to breaking Newcastle's army. Harried by the Scots horse, who picked off large numbers of stragglers, most of the recently levied Durham foot regiments dissolved, and others suffered severe losses. When Newcastle entered York on 19 April, he probably only had with him about 4,000 of his veteran infantry and 3,000 horse. On 18 April the marquis had warned the King:[30]

> ...the Scots and Fairfax having joined near Wetherby, are now too strong for us in matters of the field... they have already put themselves in such a posture as will soon ruin us, being at York, unless there is some speedy course taken to give us relief, and that with a considerable force, for their army is very strong... We shall be distressed here very shortly.

Spasmodic work to improve the defences already provided by York's medieval walls had begun during the Bishop's Wars, and continued when the city became the King's headquarters early in 1642. A series of 'sconces', or forts, linked by earthworks, had been constructed around the city.

By 16 April Leven's army had reached Thormanby, only ten miles from York. Before the enemy closed in, Newcastle sent Sir Charles Lucas out of the city, with all but about 500 of the northern cavalry. They were to harass the enemy, and then join up with any relief force.

Although the Scots had by now linked up with Lord Fairfax's army, the Allies, pending the arrival of the Earl of Manchester and the army of the Eastern Association, were too few to invest York completely. On 23 April Leven took up position on the western side of the city, with Fairfax to the east. The north and south sides were probably only covered by cavalry patrols. It was not until 3 June, after taking Lincoln, that the Eastern Association forces eventually joined the besiegers to form what was somewhat grandiloquently entitled 'the Army of Both Kingdoms'.

16. Ferdinando, 2nd Lord Fairfax (1584–1648). As a young man, Fairfax served briefly in the Low Countries, but, as his commander reported: 'he makes a tolerable country justice, but is a mere coward at fighting'. Fairfax's career as commander of the Northern Parliamentarian forces in 1642–43 would not have given much cause to alter this verdict.

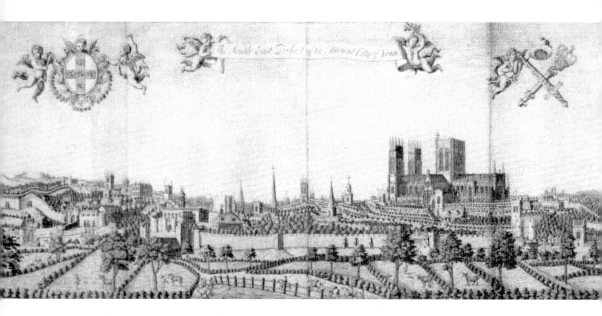

17. Southeast prospect of York, 1718.

In the interim, the besiegers had captured one Royalist outwork, but otherwise made little impact on York's resistance. Indeed the Scots were concerned by events further north, where the Marquis of Montrose, earlier grudgingly provided with a couple of hundred cavalry by Newcastle, had linked up with a small force from Cumberland and Westmorland under Col. Sir Robert Clavering, and was raiding Scots communications and outposts around Newcastle-upon-Tyne. Leven was eventually forced to detach some cavalry to counter the threat, whilst reinforcements under the Earl of Callendar which crossed the Border on 25 June were also delayed by the continuing Royalist activity in Northumberland and Durham.[31]

At York, Manchester threw a bridge of boats across the River Ouse in order to link up with the Scots, his own forces occupying a line between the Ouse and the River Fosse. During the next few days there were heavy artillery exchanges and Lord Fairfax attempted mining operations against the gate known as Walmgate Bar. This design was disclosed under torture by a captured Parliamentarian soldier, and the Royalists apparently flooded the Parliamentarian tunnel by diverting the waters of the moat into it.

Pressure increased during 6–7 June, with frequent attacks on the northern suburbs, which the Royalists unsuccessfully attempted to burn down. At the same time the Scots launched a fierce attack on the western side of the city, capturing two sconces and briefly taking a third.

Faced with this deteriorating situation, Newcastle opened negotiations, using as a pretext the fact that the Allies had omitted to send him a formal summons to surrender, and asking what their intentions were! Opinions differ on whether Newcastle's feelers had any serious intent or were merely a stalling tactic in order to gain time. The latter seems on balance to be more probable, and, if so, the Royalists won a valuable breathing space, spinning out negotiations until 15 June.

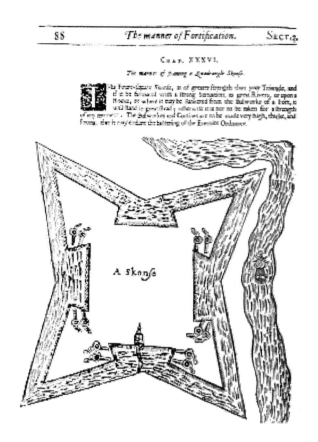

18. A 'sconce', a common type of Civil War earthen fortification.
This example is defended by artillery, and is protected on two sides by a ditch and a river.
Additional protection was often provided by a stockade and sharpened stakes known
as 'storm poles', jutting at an angle from the sides of the sconce.

On the following day the Parliamentarians launched a major assault on St Mary's Tower on the northwestern side of the city. The intention had been simultaneously to explode three mines and launch a general attack on York at several points, but, for reasons which remain obscure, Manchester's major-general of foot, Lawrence Crawford, set off his mine too soon and launched his assault prematurely. After fierce fighting, a spirited counterattack spear-headed by Newcastle's own white-coated foot regiment hurled back the attackers, with the loss of about 300 men.[32]

It was the last major action of the siege. A relative lull followed, until, on the morning of 1 July, Royalist sentries seeking to exchange customary badinage with the enemy looked down from the city walls to see the siege lines deserted. York, as they would soon discover, had been relieved.

3

'YORKE MARCH' – PRINCE RUPERT'S CAMPAIGN, FEBRUARY–1 JULY 1644

Few leading figures of the English Civil Wars have aroused more controversy than Prince Rupert of the Rhine. Aged twenty-three on the outbreak of the war, Rupert's previous military experience had been limited and less than successful, ending prematurely with his capture at the battle of Lemgo (1638). Though the prince had used his subsequent captivity in Austrian hands to embark on an intensive study of military theory, it could be argued that he owed his appointment in 1642 as Royalist general of horse more to being the King's nephew than from any evidence of military ability.

Despite his frequent association with them, it is unclear how far Rupert was personally responsible for the adoption of the 'shock' tactics, based in part on Swedish methods, which helped give the Royalist cavalry a marked superiority in the opening months of the war, but his charismatic and dynamic leadership played a major part in their success.[1]

Unfortunately, Rupert's undoubted skills as a combat commander were counterbalanced by his abrasive, intolerant and domineering personality, which led to frequent clashes with fellow officers and the King's civilian advisers. By late 1643, with tensions and recriminations brought to a new height by the failure to destroy Essex's army at Newbury, Rupert was eager to remove himself from close contact both with his enemies in the King's army and with the intrigues and disputes of the Royalist Court at Oxford. The need to find a replacement for Ormonde as commander of the 'Irish-Royalist' army in the northwest gave him the opportunity he was seeking.

On 6 January 1644 Prince Rupert was commissioned as 'captain-general' of the area currently under the temporary command of Lord Byron, and soon afterwards his appointment as President of Wales gave him control of the entire Royalist war effort in that region.

19. Prince Rupert (1619–82). Third son of Frederick V, Elector Palatine, and Elizabeth, sister of Charles I. Appointed Royalist general of horse in 1642, Rupert played an important role in the development of the Royalist cavalry and its initial successes. Under-rated as an administrator, and a capable strategist, Rupert's main weaknesses were his youth and inexperience, and his abrasive and intolerant personality.

Byron's defeat at Nantwich had left the Royalist hold on the northern part of Wales and the Marches under acute threat, and Rupert's first task was to restore the King's fortunes there, and to bring some order to a rather chaotic administrative organisation.

Setting out from Oxford for his new command on 6 February, Rupert commenced work with his customary energy and drive. Finances and garrisons were re-organised, new commanders, in many cases professional soldiers, appointed, and the final major shipment of English troops from Ireland, one cavalry and two foot regiments, totalling about 1,500 men, received, clothed and quartered at Shrewsbury.[2]

The loss of many of Byron's foot made it necessary to rebuild the Royalist field army in the northern Marches before the prince could consider offensive operations. Among the newcomers from Ireland was an experienced professional soldier, Henry Tillier, whom Rupert appointed as his major-general of foot. The two latest foot regiments to arrive, Tillier's and Robert Broughton's, along with the experienced cavalry detached from the Oxford Army, formed the core around which Rupert built his new force. At the same time, Byron at Chester was pressing conscripts from the area of his command, and exchanging prisoners in order to rebuild the regiments largely destroyed at Nantwich.[3] Following his own advice to recruit 'native' Irish in future, he also raised a regiment of foot which included a significant number of rank-and-file enlisted in Ireland, as well as officers and men from the Welsh Border.[4] The need to replace the Nantwich losses postponed the start of large-scale offensive operations by up to two months, a delay which would become of increasing significance later.

One problem facing the Royalists was the competing demands of rival generals – Rupert in the Midlands, Hopton in the south, and Forth at Oxford – for limited resources. Priority at any one time tended to be given to the currently most influential or successful commander. Fortunately for Rupert, a chance to make his mark came in March, when the vital East Midlands garrison of Newark-on-Trent was besieged by Parliamentarian forces under Sir John Meldrum. Using his own veteran cavalry and musketeers from Tillier and Broughton's regiments as the basis of a 'flying column', the prince relieved Newark on 21 March after a lightning march, and forced the surrender of Meldrum's army. It was a major victory, and, as Arthur Trevor, Rupert's agent in Oxford, pointed out to the prince:[5] 'I find no court physic so present for the opening of obstructions as good news.'

High in favour, Rupert indeed discovered that his wants met with much more prompt attention than previously, which was fortunate, as he was receiving pleas for assistance from several quarters. Apart from Newcastle's impassioned appeals for help,[6] representations were coming from the Earl of Derby, the Lancashire Royalist leader, who had been defeated in the previous year, and whose wife, the formidable Charlotte de la Tremoille, was holding out in the family home of Lathom House, under ineffectual Parliamentarian siege since February. Lathom was of little strategic importance, and not in great immediate danger, but Derby lobbied vigorously for its relief, and received grudging support from Lord Byron, who wrote from Chester to the prince on 7 April:[7]

20. Lathom House, Lancashire. The family home of the Earl of Derby, it was gallantly defended by his wife and a small garrison. The Siege of Lathom is one of the celebrated episodes of the Civil War, although Parliamentarian operations were notably inept and Lathom of only minor strategic importance.

Upon the importunity of the Lankshire gentlemen, I am forced to renue theire humble suite to Yr Highness that you would bee pleased, as soone as you are in a condition to march, to looke that way with Yr army before Latham be lost; wch they conceive may runn some hazard, if not speedily releeved upon the access of our forces to it from other parts of Lankashire. The constant intelligence from that Country every is, that if Yr Highness once appeare there, the greatest part of the Rebells forces will desert them and joyne with you, and that country beeinge once reduced, all this part of England will presently bee cleere; the rebellion in these parts beeinge wholly supported from thence...

Whensoever Yr Highness shall intend to march towards Lankashire, Yr best way from Shreusbury will bee to Whitchurch and [Market] Drayton, and thence to Knottsford [Knutsford] wch will bee a convenient place for mee to waite upon Yr Highness, with those forces I have here...

Upon the relief of Latham, Yr Highness will bee sure to have Liverpool, whereby the intercourse betwixt these parts and Ireland will bee secured, and the Rebells shipps, for want of a harbor, will not bee able to continue upon this Coast; and nothinge will more daunt the Scotts and hinder theire designes than to take the support of that country from them.

Byron's proposals would form Prince Rupert's basic strategy for the spring campaign of 1644, but various preparations were necessary before the march could get under way. During March and early April, Royalist commanders on the Welsh Border, notably Byron in the detached area of Flintshire known as Maelor Saesnig and in north Shropshire, and Sir Michael Woodhouse further south, consolidated the Cavalier position, mopping up a number of minor local Parliamentarian garrisons.

Rupert himself, in late April, paid a flying visit to Royalist headquarters at Oxford, with the object of agreeing the strategy to be followed in the south by the King whilst the prince was campaigning in the north. The Royalist position had recently worsened when Sir William Waller's victory at Cheriton (29 March) had ended any hopes of Lord Hopton's army threatening the southeast of England. Instead the King would have to stand on the defensive against the numerically superior combined armies of Waller and the Earl of Essex. Rupert proposed that the Oxford Army put the bulk of its infantry into the circle of garrisons protecting the Royalist capital, whilst the horse harried enemy communications. The prince, meanwhile, would clear Lancashire, join Newcastle and deal with the Scots and northern Parliamentarians, whilst his brother, Prince Maurice, would take the port of Lyme in Dorset. Both brothers would then link up with the King for offensive operations in the south.[8]

Despite the approval which Rupert's scheme generally receives from his biographers, its viability is questionable. The Oxford Army had insufficient foot to man adequately all of the ring of fortresses around Oxford, and its horse no longer had clear superiority over their opponents. Royalist resources were becoming increasingly stretched. A quick decision in the north by Rupert, preferably by inflicting a crushing defeat on the enemy forces, followed by a rapid march to support the King, seemed the only realistic hope of staving off defeat. It would be a gamble, with high risks, and speed would be of the essence.[9]

Knowing this, and probably harbouring doubts of the King's ability to stick to the agreed strategy, Rupert moved fast. Reports from Lancashire continued to be favourable. Lathom House still held out against a fumbling siege by Lancashire Parliamentarian forces under Col. Alexander Rigby, and Secretary of State Lord George Digby in March had assured the prince:[10] 'I do not hear, otherwise than by my Lord of Derby's servant, that the place is yet much distressed...'

The Lancashire Parliamentarian leadership were reportedly at loggerheads, their mutual distrust deepened by the failure to reduce Lathom, whose leaguer was draining their resources, with the result that Liverpool, and Warrington with its important bridge over the River Mersey, were thought each to have garrisons of only fifty men. More importantly, success in Lancashire was expected to bring in large

21. George Digby, 2nd Earl of Bristol (1612–71). A skilled political intriguer, Digby became Secretary of State to King Charles I in September 1643 after an unspectacular military career. He vied with Rupert for the King's favours for most of the remainder of the war. His intrigues and lack of integrity are generally held to have had a dire effect upon the Royalist cause.

numbers of recruits to swell the ranks of the Royalist army prior to attempting the relief of York.[11]

Disquiet over the situation in the south, as well as the increasing urgency of Newcastle's requests for assistance, forced Rupert to move slightly earlier than some of his officers would have wished. Lord Byron pondered darkly to the Earl of Ormonde:[12]

> ...this falls out unluckily for the King's affairs in these parts, in [that] the army is drawne hence, before these countryes can be reduced, but if it please God to make us successful against the Northerne Rebells, I doubt not but we shall easily prevaile against all the rest.

Rupert's contingent left Shrewsbury on 16 May, and, skirting around Parliamentarian-held Nantwich, arrived at Knutsford on 23 May.[13] It was probably here that the prince was joined by Lord Byron and the forces from Chester, bringing total Royalist strength up to about 2,600 horse and 5,000–6,000 foot.[14]

The imminent threat of attack failed to unite the squabbling Lancashire and Cheshire Parliamentarian leadership. Instead of attempting to defend in strength the crossings of the Mersey, principally at Stockport, Warrington and Hale Ford, the Lancashire forces persisted in the futile siege of Lathom, so that when Rupert appeared outside Stockport on 25 May he encountered only 3,000 men, mostly raw militia, under Col. Robert Duckenfield of the Cheshire forces.

These stood little chance against the veteran Royalist troops. A brief action took place south of the town, as Maj.-Gen. Henry Washington's Dragoons made short work of clearing the enemy musketeers out of the hedgerows and:[15]

22. Sir John Meldrum (1585–1645). A Scottish professional soldier who had served in the Low Countries and the La Rochelle Expedition of 1627–28, he also operated prior to the Civil War as an owner of lighthouses, and is said to have joined the Parliamentarian cause in order to preserve lucrative patents he had obtained. Meldrum fought at Edgehill and in 1643 served at the Siege of Hull and in Lincolnshire. He laid siege to Newark, but was defeated by Rupert (21 March 1644). He was killed during the Siege of Scarborough (1645).

...the Rebels in great affright fled towards the Towne; whom the Prince followed so close upon the heeles, that he entred pelmel with them, and so tooke the Towne, together with all their Canon, most of their Armes and Ammunition, and 800 Prisoners.

The remnants of the Parliamentarian force fell back into strongly fortified Manchester, leaving the way clear for the Royalists to cross the Mersey into Lancashire.

The Parliamentarians remained distracted. Manchester itself had recently been reinforced by a Scottish regiment, possibly detached reluctantly by the Army of Both Kingdoms before York, and commanded by Sir John Meldrum.[16] Somewhat brazenly, considering his own recent singeing at Newark from the same source, Meldrum wrote scornfully of Rupert's arrival as:[17] 'this fierce thunderbolt which strikes terror among the ignorant.'

Certainly it had a paralysing effect on the disunited committee which ran the Parliamentarian war effort in Lancashire. Col. Alexander Rigby, the leading county activist, was still at Lathom with around 2,000 men, whilst the remaining local forces were[18] 'separated and hardly to be brought together without manifest hazards.' Considerable doubts remained regarding the Royalist objective, whether it might be to attack the main Parliamentarian garrison at Manchester, move against Liverpool, or simply to gather in as many recruits as possible before heading east across the Pennines for the relief of York.

Rigby hesitated at Lathom for two critical days, undecided whether or not to head for the safety of Manchester. But, fearful that the Royalists might be heading north directly across his line of march, the Parliamentarian commander decided to take refuge in the town of Bolton until the situation clarified. It was a fatal choice.

Once Rupert had crossed the Mersey into Lancashire, the first recruits, enthusiastic if ill-armed, began to flow in to enlist under the 'exiled' Lancashire Royalists leaders the Earl of Derby, Sir Thomas Tyldesley and Lord Molyneux.[19] The Royalists made no attempt to attack Manchester, but instead swung west around the town, probably intending to relieve Lathom and pick up more recruits as they headed for Liverpool.

On the morning of 28 May, Rupert sent Maj.-Gen. Henry Tillier with one regiment of horse and one of foot to secure billets and supplies in Bolton. Tillier reported back the presence of Rigby in the town, and Rupert decided on an immediate attack.

Bolton was known as 'the Geneva of the north' because of the reputation of its inhabitants as devout Puritans. It had been the scene of some bitter fighting in the earlier stages of the war, but its defences were evidently fairly weak and neglected. They possibly consisted of little more than stone and earth 'sconces' at the main entrances to the town, perhaps with wooden gates. The defenders consisted of about 2,000 troops under Rigby, mainly musketeers together with about 500 poorly armed levies or 'clubmen'. They were reinforced by perhaps the same number of townsmen, armed with whatever was available.

At about 2 p.m., the Royalists:[20]

23. Alexander Rigby (1594–1650). A leading Lancashire Parliamentarian activist,
in 1640 Rigby was MP for Wigan, and one of the principal commanders of the Lancashire
Parliamentarian forces. He proved to be a less than inspired soldier, whose
siege of Lathom House in 1644 was both mishandled and unsuccessful.

Appeared at first like a wood or cloud, and presently were cast into severall
bodies; divers scouts appeared to discover the way for their entrance with
most advantage.

It is unclear whether Rupert summoned the defenders to surrender before ordering
an immediate assault. Calling a council of war, he,[21] 'Rightly judged [Bolton] would
make a vigorous resistance'. The attack was mounted at several points by the foot
regiments of Robert Ellis, Sir Thomas Tyldesley, Henry Warren and Prince Rupert.
The first two of these probably included a high proportion of raw levies, and, already
hindered by a heavy downpour of rain, they met with desperate resistance. A
Parliamentarian account claimed:[22]

Our Commanders were very courageous, and our Souldiers very hardy, and
both resolved to stand to it, and in the first encounter gave them about halfe
an houres' sharpe entertainment, were close in discharge, as the enemies
confessed after, and repulsed them bravely to the enemies' great losse and
discoragement, and in their retreate cut them downe before them in great
abundance, and they fell like leaves from the tree on a winter morning.

According to the Royalists, Warren and Rupert's men, under heavy fire from muskets and cannon, failed to penetrate the defences; Ellis and Tyldesley gained entry to the town, but were thrown back in a counterattack by a troop of Lancashire horse under Col. Nicholas Shuttleworth.

Losses were fairly severe, totalling 200–300 men; Lt-Col. John Russell of Rupert's regiment of foot was wounded, and his major was captured.[23]

Shuttleworth's horse were in turn driven back by Royalist cavalry, the Earl of Derby reportedly capturing an enemy cornet,[24] and an uneasy lull followed.

Exactly what happened next has been the subject of some dispute, but it seems that the defenders unwisely chose to execute in full view of the attackers a Royalist captured in the assault, 'and hung him up as an Irish Papist'.[25] This ill-judged action may well have been the responsibility of the hard-line Alexander Rigby, but it served only to infuriate the Royalists. 'Highly provoked', Prince Rupert called a second council of war, and ordered a renewed assault, forbidding 'quarter to any person then in arms'.

The only fresh unit available was Robert Broughton's regiment from Ireland, but it was supported by two companies of Tyldesley's men, with whom the Earl of Derby served as a volunteer. The biased account of events by Seacombe gives Derby credit for the success of the attack:[26]

> The Earl of Derby with his two hundred men marched directly to the Walls, and after Quarter of an Hour's hot dispute, Entered the First Man himself, who being Bravely Seconded by fresh supplies the Towne was instantly attack'd on every Quarter.

It seems in fact that a key role was played by a party of horse, who, possibly with the aid of a Royalist sympathiser inside Bolton, found an unguarded entrance and took the Parliamentarians in the rear. 'There could be no resistance almost made',[27] and the defenders began to break, many of them fleeing towards the surrounding countryside.

Some vicious street fighting followed, as the Royalist horse scoured the streets, driving the defenders back towards the church and market place in the centre of the town. The alleged 'Bolton Massacre' would take its place in the forefront of Civil War atrocities, with lurid reports in Parliamentarian news sheets of the wholesale slaughter of unarmed men, women and children. It continues to hold such a dubious distinction even in modern accounts, and so the reality is worth examining. Rupert's order, to forbid 'quarter to any person then in arms', was fairly common practice when assaulting a town, particularly if a summons to surrender had been rejected, though we have no evidence that such an ultimatum had been issued at Bolton. Certainly there was considerable killing of the defenders as resistance degenerated into a rout. During this, there must inevitably have been some civilian casualties, though there is only documented evidence of four women, and no children, being killed. The Bolton Parish Register, which might be expected to have recorded the burials of any townspeople, lists only these four women, together with the names of

24. James Stanley, 7th Earl of Derby (1607–51). His standing as the leading Lancashire magnate and landowner made Derby the natural choice to command the King's supporters in the county. But, an uninspired general, and short of men and resources, Derby quickly lost ground, and by the summer of 1643 only Lathom House and Greenhaugh Castle were still held by the Royalists. After holding out in the Isle of Man, in 1651 Derby joined Charles II's unsuccessful invasion of England, was captured, and was executed for his alleged role in the 'Bolton Massacre'.

seventy-eight men of the town, many of whom were probably actively involved in the defence of Bolton.

The Earl of Derby would later be accused of the murder in cold blood of a former servant of his, Capt. William Bootle, but, although Bootle was certainly killed in the fighting, Derby always strenuously denied the charge, and the exact circumstances of Bootle's death remain unclear. Most of the verifiable ill-treatment seems to have consisted of rough handling and insults, rather than widespread killing, and widespread looting, which were the inevitable accompaniment to the storm of any enemy garrison.[28]

About 700 of the defenders, probably mostly townsmen, took refuge in the church, and were granted quarter. Rigby himself was fortunate enough to overhear the Royalist field word, and passing himself off as one of Rupert's officers, slipped out of the town and gained the safety of Manchester. In all the Parliamentarians seem to have lost about 1,000 dead in the town and surrounding fields, and 600 prisoners, together with twenty-three colours and a large quantity of arms and ammunition.

25. Blau's Map of Lancashire, 1648.

Rupert made no attempt to garrison Bolton, but, sending the captured colours to the safekeeping of the Countess of Derby at Lathom, turned his attention to his principal objective in Lancashire, the port of Liverpool.

The fall of Bolton, and the lurid tales of Royalist atrocities there, threw the Parliamentarians into still greater confusion. Although in theory there were estimated to be twelve troops of horse and 7,000 foot available in Lancashire,[29] they were dispersed over a wide area and lacked experienced officers and supplies. Sir John Meldrum recommended to the Committee of Both Kingdoms that they be reinforced by troops from the army before York, together with Lord Denbigh's forces from the Midlands. On 1 June the Committee made a similar recommendation to the commanders at York, but the latter refused to dilute their strength in this way, and Rupert was left to continue his operations undisturbed.[30]

Still recruiting, Rupert was joined on 4 June at Bury by George Goring, now back in post as Newcastle's general of horse, with 5,000 northern and Newark horse (including the troops under Lucas sent out of York) and 800 Derbyshire foot, who had skirmished their way across the Midlands. Though 'not soe well appointed as expected', they brought with them large herds of looted cattle.

Advance parties of Royalist horse and dragoons appeared before Liverpool on 6 June, with the main army arriving next day.

Liverpool was a town of about 1,000 inhabitants, standing on the east bank of the River Mersey. The town had been in Royalist hands until the spring of 1643, when it passed probably bloodlessly under Parliamentarian control. A local land-owner and MP, Col. John Moore, was made governor, and work began on strengthening the defences. The eastern side of Liverpool was partially protected by an inlet of the Mersey known as the 'Pool', and this was supplemented by other works. They followed the usual contemporary pattern, consisting of earthen ramparts with 'mounts' at intervals. In front of the ramparts was a ditch, 36ft wide and 9ft deep, which ran from north of a house known as the Old Hall to the northern edge of the Pool. There were gates through the ramparts, strengthened by cannon, at the ends of Old Hall Street, Dale Street and Tithebarn Street. Additional earthworks and batteries were constructed to cover the approaches to the Pool, with particularly strong defences based around the medieval castle.

Though Liverpool's fortifications were reasonably good, the town was overlooked by a ridge of high ground, Everton Heights, to the east, which dropped quite steeply towards the river.

In June 1644, the earth defences had been further bolstered by an inner lining of woolpacks, intended to absorb the effects of artillery fire. The garrison, perhaps 1,000 in all, still commanded by Moore, consisted of his own fairly weak foot regiment, about 400 Scots troops sent by Meldrum, a small number of seamen from the Parliamentarian ships in the harbour, and such citizens who were deemed trust-worthy to bear arms. Many non-combatants had already been sent out of town.[31]

Two summons to surrender were rejected, on the second occasion the Royalist trumpeter having his horse shot from under him. Although Prince Rupert report-edly commented, probably for morale-boosting purposes, that Liverpool was 'a

26. Liverpool in 1680. The castle is on the right and St Nicholas' Church on the left
of the picture. The fortification by the river is the Tower, belonging to the Earls of Derby.
Note the dominating Everton Heights (background), where the Royalist siege camp was sited.

nest of crows that a party of boys might take', the strength of the defences made
another quick success like that at Bolton unlikely, and the Royalists began
constructing siegeworks.

Emplacements were built for at least three heavy guns, probably in the area now
occupied by St George's Plateau, and a continuous artillery bombardment
commenced, as the besiegers gradually extended their trenches closer to the defences.[32]

The matter was disputed very hotly until the tenth day of June with musket
and great shott without measure out of the towne and from the shipps, upon
which day our line approached within a coites cast of the gate where our great
shott had almost filled the ditch with the ruines of the sodd wall, and about
noone a furious assaulte was made by our menn where a terrible fight was on
both sides above the space of an houre upon the workes, the Enemy resolute,
ours not seconded retreated with some losse.

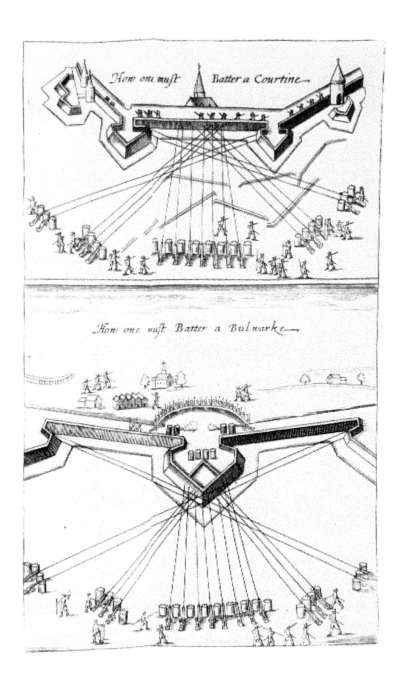

27. Contemporary diagrams showing the correct positioning
of siege batteries to open breaches in fortifications.

The Parliamentarians, in what was certainly a gross exaggeration, claimed to have inflicted 1,500 casualties on the attackers. Rupert was probably less concerned about the men lost, who were replaceable, than with the expenditure of large quantities of scarce powder and ammunition.

However the defences of Liverpool were beginning to crumble under the continued remorseless bombardment. At about midnight on 11 June, in an act which blackened his name thereafter among the citizens of Liverpool, John Moore and his officers, with some of their men, quietly abandoned their positions, leaving twelve colours flying from the walls as a deception, and, with as much of their personal property as they could carry, took refuge on ships in the harbour.[33]

> Which Collonell Tillyer perceivinge, having the Guarde next the Sea [at the north end of the town] supposeing the Enemy to bee gone, entred the Towne with little or noe resistance, found about 400 of the meaner sorte of menne, wherof most were killed, some had quarter.

28. Siege guns; culverin top and demi-cannon below. Note the alternative types of firing platforms constructed from planks and woven branches, which were necessary to prevent guns sinking into the ground as a result of recoil.

29. Caryl Molyneux served as lieutenant-colonel to his brother, Richard, Lord Molyneux. The five hands in his cornet refer to the 'Five Members' of Parliament regarded as the leading opponents of the King. The stag was the emblem of the Earl of Essex, and the motto translates as 'To What [Purpose] Do You Praise This Horn'.

According to Byron, the assault was made by the Red Regiment (possibly Tillier's), guided by Lt-Col. Caryl Molyneux, an officer with local knowledge, who reputedly killed seven or eight men with his own hand. In all, about 360 of the defenders, including a number of non–combatants, seem to have been killed in the panic and confusion of the night attack before Rupert entered the town and granted quarter. The Scottish troops, formed up to fight near the castle, obtained terms, whilst the town was thoroughly pillaged.[34]

Will Legge, Governor of Chester, expressed Royalist satisfaction at the victory when he wrote to Ormonde on 13 June:[35] 'And now Liverpool is in our hands, I hope that we shall have a freer intelligence from Ireland than before we had. I assure that was the end we stopped there for.' In practice, however, the Parliamentarian naval squadron, which had escaped capture, quickly established a blockade of the port.

Royalist losses at Liverpool are unknown, but can hardly have been lighter than those suffered at Bolton. More serious was the expenditure of 100 barrels of powder. The need to await new supplies, which had to be brought overland by convoy, often threatened by enemy attack, from the Royalist magazines at Bristol and Worcester, other than any limited quantities available from Chester and Shrewsbury, was one of the main reasons for the pause in operations which followed. In fact, it is hard to see that the Royalists could have gained any particular advantage from moving to the relief of York any earlier. Rupert also needed time to organise further recruits and set in train the re-fortification of Liverpool and Lathom House.

30. King Charles I (1600–49). His failure to follow the strategy agreed with Prince Rupert
in the spring of 1644, however justified, placed the King in serious danger, and led him
to send the prince a letter decisive in his resolution to bring the Allies to battle after
the Relief of York.

Unfortunately, events elsewhere forced his hand. As Rupert had half-expected, the King abandoned the agreed southern strategy. The garrisons of Reading and Abingdon, both key elements of the outer defences of Oxford, were evacuated in the face of the threat of Essex and Waller's armies. There were good reasons for this decision; neither could have withstood determined attack, and their troops were of more use reinforcing the foot of the Oxford Army than as prisoners.

However the loss of these outposts enabled Essex and Waller to close in on Oxford itself, and the King, with his cavalry and some foot, was forced to flee from the threatened Royalist capital over the Cotswolds to Worcester. On 6 June, Essex and Waller, in one of the more ill-judged decisions of the war, threw away their chance of ending the conflict within days by dividing their forces. Essex would head west to relieve Lyme, whilst Waller would be left to deal with the King.

It would, however, be some time before King Charles became aware of the improvement in his fortunes, and on 14 June he despatched to Rupert a fateful letter. The implications of what he wrote will be looked at more closely in the next chapter, but the phrase which made the greatest impression on the prince was that which read:[36]

> ...if York be relieved, and you beat the rebel's army of both kingdoms, which are before it, then (but otherwise not) I may possibly make a shift (upon the defensive) to spin out time until you come to assist me.

Rupert was evidently furious, and, blaming the machinations of the King's councillors, briefly considered throwing up his command.[37] But loyalty to his uncle, and increasing concerns that the negotiations which Newcastle had begun with the Allied commanders before York might result in the surrender of the city convinced the prince of the need to move quickly.

Sir Robert Byron was made Governor of Liverpool, and left with a garrison consisting of his own veteran regiment (which might have been more valuable as part of the field army), and a newly raised unit commanded by Col. Cuthbert Clifton. Then Rupert, with perhaps 7,000 horse, 6,000 foot and sixteen guns,[38] set off on the first stage of his 'Yorke Marche'.

Rupert reached Preston on 23 June. He pushed on to Clitheroe on the following day, taking a small nearby Parliamentarian garrison en route, and then, after installing one of his officers, Col. Thomas Daniel, as Governor of Clitheroe, reached Skipton Castle on 26 June.[39]

Here the Royalists halted for three days, to 'fixe our armes',[40] carry out some last-minute drilling of the recruits obtained in Lancashire, and absorb perhaps 1,000 horse from Cumberland and Westmoreland. Messengers were also despatched to ascertain the current situation at York, and inform Newcastle of Rupert's approach.

For their part, the Allied generals had been viewing Rupert's operations in Lancashire with increasing concern. They had informed the Committee of Both Kingdoms on 5 June that they felt it unsafe to divide their forces by sending part to encounter Rupert in Lancashire:[41]

> If we should raise our siege before York, and march with all our forces against him, it is in his discretion to avoid us, and either pass by another way than that we take, and so come into Yorkshire, or else retire into Cheshire, whither if we should pursue him, it would be in the Marquis of Newcastle's power in our absence to recover all Yorkshire again and increase his army to as great strength as ever it was. Therefore we have all of us resolved it be the most convenient to quarter our horse and dragoons betwixt Ripon and Otley and some other forces about Blackstone Edge to stop the enemy's suddenly falling upon these parts, or raising our siege, which is especially intended by them, and in the meantime we shall continue our siege here and attempt what is possible for the gaining of the place, and then we may pursue Prince Rupert with our united forces, or, if he make his passage sooner into Yorkshire, then we must draw off our forces from before the town and joining all our forces together, give him a field, wherein, if it pleases God to bless us with victory,

all the county of Lancashire and the City of York also will in all probability fall of themselves to us.

There was a good deal of sense in this plan, even if the Allies, particularly the Scots and the Earl of Manchester, were as much motivated by a desire not to expose their own communications and home territories by venturing west of the Pennines. They also optimistically hoped that the King's deteriorating position might force Rupert to turn south without even attempting to relieve York.

The Parliamentarian defeat in Lancashire reinforced the Allied generals in their strategy. They were hoping for reinforcements both from Lancashire and the Earl of Denbigh's Midlands forces. But the latter had only about 1,800 men, semi-mutinous through lack of pay, and seems to have made no serious effort to carry out the Committee of Both Kingdom's instructions to link up with the forces before York.[42] About 1,500 Lancashire horse and foot, under Col. George Dodding, did reach the army at York ahead of Prince Rupert.

On 23 June, Sir Henry Vane, the Committee of Both Kingdom's representative with the Allied forces before York, wrote to Westminster:[43]

> Prince Rupert with all his foot and horse, about 11,000, has his rendezvous this night at Preston, which looks this way, though it be conceived he will not advance yet awhile, which makes it very questionable whether we should go and attack him in Lancashire, blocking up this city still, or stay until he come into Yorkshire nearer to us; to which I find little other resolution than to wait upon the occasion, and to do as they [the commanders] shall find cause upon fresh intelligence one way or other… we hope if Lord Denbigh make haste, we may be able to attempt upon Prince Rupert without raising the siege here or staying for his attempting upon us.

On 29 June, Rupert resumed his advance, marching via Denton to Knaresborough, which he reached next day. It was clear to the Allied commanders that their hoped-for reinforcements would not reach them before the Royalists were upon them, and on 30 June they decided to lift the siege of York and concentrate their forces in an attempt to prevent Rupert and Newcastle from linking up.

During the night of 30 June/1 July the Allies abandoned their siege lines and took up position astride the York–Knaresborough road, deployed northwest of the village of Long Marston, seven miles west of York, with the River Nidd forming a barrier between themselves and Rupert's forces. Here they could not only block any Royalist approach along the Knaresborough road, but also guard the road from Wetherby and keep open their communications with the West Riding, Hull and the Eastern Association (though the Scots were in a less fortunate position). A bridge of boats at Poppleton, guarded by Manchester's dragoons, would enable the Allies to switch troops to the eastern bank of the Ouse. They still hoped to be joined in the next day or so by Denbigh and Meldrum, and would then have marked superiority in numbers with which to give Rupert battle.

Rupert, with a fair idea of the Allies' total strength of about 27,000 men, had no desire to face them in battle until he had linked up with Newcastle's troops from York. The Allied deployment at Long Marston effectively closed to him both the direct route from Knaresborough and the road from Wetherby. Instead he chose to make a wide left hook and approach York from the northwest, in a 32-mile march from Knaresborough to Galtres Forest, via Boroughbridge and Thornton Bridge.

The main danger was that if the Allies discovered the move in time, they might cross the Ouse by the bridge of boats at Poppleton and block Rupert's advance. So, in a feint, early on 1 July the prince sent a strong cavalry force up the Knaresborough road to face the Allies drawn up on Marston Moor. Believing the horse to be the vanguard of Rupert's army, the Allied generals drew up for battle.

But as the hours passed with no sign of the Royalist main force, it gradually became clear to Leven and his fellow generals that they had been deceived. The road from Boroughbridge to York, along which Rupert was marching, had been left completely unguarded by the enemy, possibly when, at 1.30 a.m., Oliver Cromwell, Manchester's lieutenant-general of horse, had urged that scattered units of Lord Fairfax's army which were stationed in that area be concentrated with the main armies.[44]

31. Musketeer wearing a version of the popular 'montero' cap.
He carries his ammunition in about a dozen wooden powder chargers suspended
from a bandolier, which also has a powder flask and bullet bag attached.

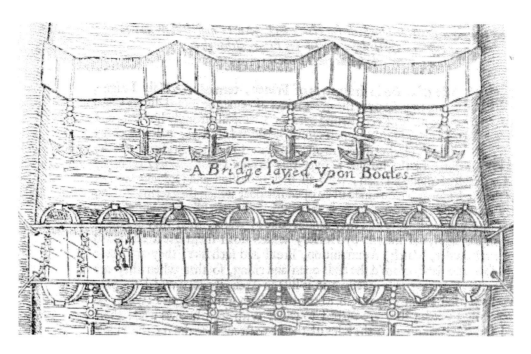

32. Contemporary engraving of the type of bridge of boats
employed by the Allied armies on the River Ouse at Poppleton.

As a result, Royalist cavalry were able to surprise and drive off Manchester's dragoons guarding the bridge of boats at Poppleton, three miles northwest of York, and Rupert's men crossed the Ouse without opposition.

In one of the most skilful operations of the war, the Allies had been completely out-manoeuvred, and York relieved. The initiative lay in Royalist hands, and the entire outcome of the war might well hang on the decisions made by Rupert and Newcastle during the next few hours.

4

MARSTON MOOR:
OPENING MOVES,
1 July–Noon 2 July

Soon after dawn on 1 July, finding the Allied siege lines apparently deserted, Newcastle sent a party of horse out of York down the Selby road to investigate. Near Fulwood they clashed briefly with enemy cavalry covering the withdrawal of Lord Fairfax's army over the Ouse.[1] It was clear that the siege had been lifted, but it was probably not until about noon that Newcastle had definite information when 'Captain [Robert] Legg brought news of the prince's approach.'[2] Newcastle responded with a fulsome letter of gratitude to his deliverer:[3]

> You are welcome so manye severall wayes, as itt is beyond my Arethmetick to number, but this I knowe you are the redemer of the North and the saviour of the Crowne. Your name Sir hath terefide the great Generalls and they flye before itt. Itt seems theyr designe is nott to meet your Highnesse for I believe they have gott a river betweene you and them butt they are so newlye gone as ther is [no] certaintie att all of them or their intentions, neyther can I resolve any thinges since I am made of nothinge butt thankfulnesse and obedience to your Highness commands.

This epistle was vintage Newcastle, courtly, elaborate and probably both irritating and irrelevant to the matter-of-fact Rupert. It told him little of use concerning enemy movements or Newcastle's own intentions. The prince may, however, have taken Newcastle's final sentence at face value, and assumed that the marquis was indeed putting himself unreservedly under Rupert's orders.

Given Newcastle's well-attested distrust of both the prince and Court circles, and his concern to preserve the dignities of his own independent command, this was a highly questionable assumption to have made. Indeed the Royalist command situation was now both complicated and unclear. Sir Hugh Cholmley would later claim that Rupert had been given a commission to command both Royalist armies, and that Newcastle's independent authority was at an end,[4] but there is no surviving documentary evidence to confirm this. Both the prince and Newcastle held the rank of captain-general over clearly defined geographical areas, which overlapped in the case of Lancashire and Cheshire. But Newcastle had never exerted active command of these counties, and there is nothing to suggest that Rupert had clear authority in the heartlands of Newcastle's territory. His seniority, if any, would have rested on his royal birth, which did not automatically bestow such a right. It would have been typical of King Charles to have avoided coming down on either side in such a contentious matter, and to have left the situation unclear. If so, it would prove to be a costly omission.

The Royalist vanguard pushed on through the afternoon, halting to snatch a few hours' rest that evening in Galtres Forest. Perhaps Rupert could have seized the opportunity for a face-to-face meeting with Newcastle, but, possibly feeling his presence was needed with his own troops, or shunning such a confrontation, he failed to do so. Both generals may also have felt that making the first move towards a meeting would have been an admission of the other's authority. It was an unfortunate display of personal distrust and animosity which would have far-reaching consequences. Instead of entering York himself, at some point that evening Rupert sent Newcastle's general of horse, George Goring, into York with terse instructions to the marquis to bring the northern troops out of the city to join him on Marston Moor by 4 a.m. next morning.

There is a good deal of controversy concerning exactly what happened in York during the next few hours. It seems that Newcastle was offended by Rupert's attitude, and his discontent was fanned by some of his officers, especially his treasurer at war, Lord Widdrington, and Lord Eythin, whose old quarrel with Rupert dating back to the incident at Lemgo in 1638 was rankling again. There was, however, a deeper consideration going beyond personal animosity. As we shall see later, both Newcastle and Eythin were opposed to bringing on the battle with the Allies which Rupert's orders implied to be his intention. They claimed to be confident that the Army of Both Kingdoms would shortly break apart of its own accord, and were expecting further Royalist reinforcements from the north. Newcastle was also keenly aware that the foot with him in York were effectively the last of his Northern Army. If they were destroyed, his command would, for practical purposes, die with them.

Newcastle, however,[5] 'Immediately sent some persons of quality to attend His Highness, and to invite him into the city to consult...'

In the meantime he apparently began to make preparations to follow Rupert's wishes, pointing out that it would take some time to clear one of the city gates of the earth and other obstacles used to block it during the siege. Many of the foot had absented themselves during the afternoon in order to loot the abandoned Allied camp and would, Newcastle claimed, take some time to re-muster.

At this point Lord Eythin took a hand. The governor of York Castle (Clifford's Tower), Sir Francis Cobbe, supposedly later told Rupert that Eythin actively attempted to dissuade the marquis from following the prince's orders.[6]

33. Clifford's Tower (York Castle) in 1680.

...all the foot were at 2 a-clock that night drawn in a body expecting to march out of the city, when there came an order from General King [Eythin], that they should not march till they had their pay whereupon they all quitt theire colours and disperst. This I had from a gentleman of quality of that country, who was a colonel and had a command there and was present at that time. But in justification of King, some say that there was not half the foot, for many of them being plundering in the enemy's trenches where they found good booty, they could not be drawn together so soon; true it is many were wandering, yet doubtless there was a considerable number; again King denies he sent any such message, but that it being pay day the soldiers would not out of the city without it and raised this of themselves; certainly a report was divulged that King sent such an order, from whencesoever it came, and that disperst the soldiers.[7]

Certainly it seems that Eythin did little to enforce Rupert's orders; apart from his doubts regarding their wisdom, he may well have been reluctant to face his fellow countrymen in battle. 'Strikes' on the eve of battle, with soldiers refusing to march until their grievances had been met, were not unusual on the Continent. Eythin would have been well aware of the practice, and could have ensured that the idea was passed to receptive ears. The end result was that Royalist strategy was beginning to unravel.

In the opposing camp, the Allied generals, their own plans in disarray, had called a council of war on the evening of 1 July. It seems to have been a fairly acrimonious session. Leven, by virtue of leading the largest contingent of the Army of Both Kingdoms, was acting as commander-in-chief, but it soon became clear that the Allies were working to somewhat differing agendas. It was eventually decided to pull back from Marston Moor. Leven argued that Meldrum and Denbigh and their rein-forcements could be expected to reach Wakefield on 5 July, and that it would be wisest to avoid battle until they arrived. In the meantime, the Allies would fall back southwards through Cawood to strategically placed Selby:[8]

> ...partly to possess the River [Ouse] intending, so to hinder him [Rupert] from furnishing Yorke with provisions, out of the East Riding; also to interpose between him and his march southwards, he having no other way to march (the Earl of Denbigh and the Lancashire forces interposing between him and his march Westwards, the way he came.)

The Allied troops spent a fairly miserable night:[9] 'very few had either the comfort of convenient roofs, or food: our Souldiers did drink the Wells dry, and then were necessitated to make use of puddle water.'

However it might be rationalised, the decision was in fact a retreat, and certainly had the potential to lead to the break-up of the Army of Both Kingdoms, as well as giving back control of much of northern Yorkshire to the Royalists.

> ...upon Tuesday morning, a partie of the enemies horse having faced us awhile, wheeled back out of sight, which gave us cause to suspect that the maine body was marched towards Tadcaster... where he might cut off the river, and so both scant us of provisions and get down suddainly into the South.[10]
>
> Accordingly, early in the morning, wee began our march towards Cawood, with all our Armee, leaving three thousand Horse and Dragoons to bringe up the Reare of our Foote and Ordnance.[11]

It was probably about 9 a.m. when the Scots in the van of the march had 'got almost to Tadcaster', and the Eastern Association foot, in the rear, were 'two or three miles from Marston', that the Allied generals, marching with the column, received 'a very hot alarm', that Royalist horse were appearing in strength on Marston Moor.

The Allied rearguard consisted of about 3,000 horse under Cromwell, David Leslie and Sir Thomas Fairfax. They were positioned on the ridge of high ground to the south of Marston Moor, from where they could observe the approach roads from York. There was a clear danger that the Royalists might go on to occupy the ridge and then attack the marching Allied columns. Sir Thomas Fairfax explained:[12] 'We [himself, Leslie and Cromwell] sent word to the Generalls of the necessity of making a stand.'

Though there was still no sign of Newcastle and his troops, Rupert had got his own men on the march at the first glimmer of daylight. By 4 a.m. on 2 July his

34. Oliver Cromwell (1599–1658). Member of Parliament for Huntingdon from 1628,
Cromwell seems to have undergone a religious conversion in about 1636, and became
a leading member of the Puritan movement. Aged forty-three on the outbreak of Civil War,
he quickly became known for his success in raising, training and motivating cavalry.
After his successes in 1643 at Grantham, Gainsborough and Winceby, he was appointed
lieutenant-general of horse in the Army of the Eastern Association, but his rise to military
prominence really dates from Marston Moor.

leading cavalry units were filing across the bridge of boats at Poppleton heading for
Marston Moor. They found the Allied position on the moor unoccupied, but the
ridge to the south held by the Allied cavalry rearguard.

Skirmishing seems to have begun at about 9 a.m., Rupert's leading cavalry
hoping to drive their opponents from their dominating position. A Parliamentarian
account explained:[13]

On Tuesday the second of July we pitch in Hessam-Moore, where no sooner
looking about us, but the enemy with displayed coloures entered the same
place bending towards the left hand by some reason of advantage they
perceived there; which we striving to prevent, made for it, before they should
possess themselves of it; in the meantime [their] main body... pitcht in that
place and neere unto it which we left...

The Allied cavalry commanders, realising how vital possession of the ridge was, resolved[14] 'to make it good until they [the foot] came back to us.'

The Allied horse were most likely in position on the forward slopes of the ridge south of the Long Marston-Tockwith road, roughly between Tockwith on the left and the Atterwith Enclosures to the right. The Royalist aim was to gain possession of the same ground, as well as the ridge line beyond, and, as the first of their infantry, probably a brigade consisting of Prince Rupert's and Lord Byron's regiments, appeared, an attempt was made to push the enemy cavalry back from their advantageous position.[15]

> The Enemy perceiving that our Cavalry had possessed themselves of a corn hill, and having discovered neer unto that hill a place of great advantage, where they might have Sun and Wind of us, advanced thither with a Regiment of Red Coats, and a party of Horse.

The disputed ground was probably just to the southeast of the village of Tockwith, and consisted of a barely perceptible piece of rising ground and a large man-made rabbit warren known as Bilton Bream.

Cromwell's Eastern Association cavalry, who formed the left wing of the Allied covering force:[16] 'sent out a party which beat them off, and planted there our left wing of Horse.' It was probably during this skirmishing that the Royalists suffered their first recorded casualty of the battle, when:[17]

> ...the enemy makes some shot as they were drawing up into Battalio, and ye first shot kills [Roger Houghton] a sonne of Sir Gilbert Houghton that was captain in ye Prince's Army [he served in Lord Molyneux's regiment of horse].

The deploying Royalist horse had possibly come under fire from enemy dragoons in the Bilton Bream area. The failure to secure Bilton Bream had been the Royalists' first significant setback, and Cholmley was anxious to shift the blame from the prince himself:[18]

> The Princes' Army ere ever he was aware, was drawn too near the enemy, and into some place of disadvantage, which may be imputed to his commanders that had the leading and marshalling of his forces than to himself.

By implication Byron and perhaps Tillier are indicted, but this 'special pleading' remains unconvincing. The preliminary skirmishing lasted for much of the morning, and it seems unlikely that Rupert was not among the first Royalist troops to reach the scene, as well as playing a leading part in planning their deployment. Royalist difficulties arose as a result of the decision of the Allied cavalry commanders to stand firm on the ridge, and their success in denying their opponents – who attacked piecemeal as units came up – control of the advantageous ground around Bilton

Bream. As a result the Royalists were forced to deploy on the open moor, about 500 yards north of the ridge.

It is clear that for much of the morning Rupert hoped to be able to launch a full-scale attack on the ridge before the Allied foot returned in strength. However he felt that he needed the northern foot to ensure success, and was, of course, still expecting their imminent arrival:[19]

> [He] would have attaqued ye Enemy himself in their Retreat, [but] if ye Prince had fallen upon ye Rear and miscarried it would have been objected that he should have stayed for Newcastle.

As his own men came up, Rupert and his officers deployed them, and:[20] 'by divers regiments of muskettiers so lined the hedge and ditch betwixt his position and the ridge [that] our Souldiers could not assault them without very great apparent prejudice.'

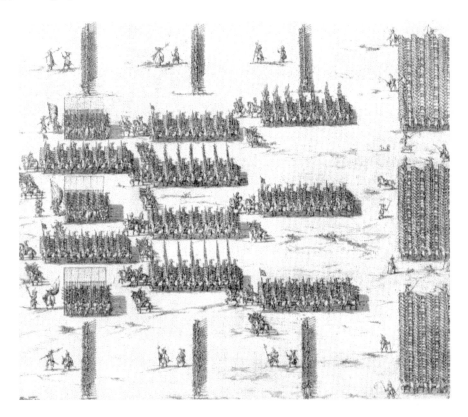

35. Contemporary engraving of an army deploying for battle. The process, normally carried out in accordance with a pre-determined battle plan, could be lengthy and involved, particularly with poorly trained troops. At Marston Moor it continued at intervals for much of the day.

The Royalists were probably detaching parties of 'commanded' musketeers from each foot regiment as it came up, and reinforcing them with Henry Washington's dragoons and at least six light guns. But until the northern foot arrived, the Royalist infantry would be spread thin, and unable to take the offensive. Throughout the morning Rupert's impatience mounted, and he was[21] 'sending away to my Lord Newcastle to march with all speed' and 'sent messages to ye Earle from time to time'.

Rupert's urgency was not matched in York. It was probably as late as 9 a.m. before Newcastle himself left the city, choosing, with perhaps significant lack of haste for such a celebrated horseman, to travel in his coach, escorted by his lifeguard of horse. It may have been noon before he eventually met up with Rupert somewhere on Marston Moor. The prince controlled his normally fiery temper with some evident difficulty:[22] 'My Lord, I wish you had come sooner with your forces, but I hope we shall yet have a glorious day.'

36. A Scots dragoon. He is dressed much like his infantry counterpart in hodden grey, apart from his riding boots. Given the evidence that many of Newcastle's infantry were also issued with blue bonnets, he also resembles some of the foot of the Royalist Northern Army.

Newcastle's response can have done nothing to improve Rupert's mood. The northern foot, he announced, had been,[23]

> ...plundering in the enemy's trenches and that it was impossible to have got them together at the time prefixed, but that he had left General King about the work, who would bring them up with all the expedition that might be.

Rupert was probably near-frantic as he saw his advantage slipping away, and[24] 'would with his own foot have been falling on the enemy, but that the Marquis dissuaded him, telling him that he had 4,000 as good foot as were in World.'

Newcastle, as we shall see, was certainly over-estimating the number of infantry he had available, and even his inflated total may have disappointed Rupert, who possibly expected 10,000 men from York.[25] As the discussion between the Royalist commanders continued, it became increasingly evident that they disagreed sharply regarding the best strategy to be adopted.[26]

> ...after some conferences, he [Newcastle] declared his mind to the Prince, desiring his Highness not to attempt anything as yet upon the enemy; for he had intelligence that there was some discontent between them, and that they were resolved to divide themselves, and so to raise the siege without fighting; besides my Lord expected within two days Colonel Cleavering with above three thousand drawn out of several garrisons (who also came at the same time, though it was then too late). But his Highness answered my lord, that he had a letter from his Majesty with a positive and absolute command to fight the enemy; which in obedience, and according to his duty he was bound to perform. Whereupon my Lord replied: That he was ready and willing, for his part, to obey his Highness in all things, no otherwise than if his Majesty was in person there himself, and though several of my Lord's friends advised him not to engage in battle, because the command, (as they said) was taken from him; yet my Lord answered them, that happen what would, he would not shun to fight, for he had no other ambition but to live and die a loyal subject to his Majesty.

This debate was decisive in what followed. Newcastle was undoubtedly guilty of some special pleading, although there was a basis of truth in his claims regarding Allied discord. He did however considerably exaggerate the strength of the troops under Clavering, who actually numbered about 1,300 horse.[27] It seems clear that he and Eythin remained determined to avoid battle if at all possible, whether from a genuine belief that the Allied forces would break up of their own accord, or because of their fear of defeat and the destruction of the northern forces which would follow.

For his part, Rupert made his letter from the King his justification. In the absence of any evidence for the existence of any other command, this letter must be taken to be that of 14 June, so vital in its influence on events which followed, which was mentioned earlier, and which now deserves to be quoted in full:[28]

37. Micklegate Bar, York. This had been blocked up during the siege, and Newcastle gave the need to clear it as an excuse for the delay of the Northern foot in reaching Marston Moor.

Nephew,

First, I must congratulate with you for your good successes, assuring you that the things themselves are no more welcome to me than that you are the means. I know the importance of the supplying you with powder, for which I have taken all possible ways, having sent both to Ireland and Bristol. As from Oxford, this bearer is well satisfied that it is impossible to have at present; but if he tells you that I can spare them from thence, I leave you to judge, having but thirty-six [barrels] left. But what I can get from Bristol (of which there is not much certainty it being threatened to be besieged) you shall have.

But now I must give you the true state of my affairs, which if their condition enforces me to give you more peremptory commands than I would willingly do, you must not take it ill. If York be lost I shall esteem my crown little less, unless supported by your sudden march to me; and a miraculous conquest in the South, before the effects of their Northern power can be found here. But if York be relieved, and you beat the rebels army of both kingdoms, which are before it; then (but otherwise not) I may possibly make a shift upon the defensive to spin out time until you come to assist me. Wherefore I command and conjure you, by the duty and affection which I know you bear me, that all new enterprises laid aside, you immediately march, according to your first intention, with all your force to the relief of York. But if that be either lost, or have freed themselves from the besiegers, or that, for want of powder, you cannot undertake that work, that you imme-diately march with your whole strength, directly to Worcester, to assist me and my army; without which, or your having relieved York by beating the Scots, all the successes you can afterwards have must infallibly be useless unto me. You may believe that nothing but an extreme necessity could make me write thus unto you; wherefore, in this case, I can no ways doubt of your punctual compliance with.

Your loving uncle and most faithful friend,
Charles R.

Much debate has centred around the exact meaning of the King's letter, the sugges-tion often being made that Rupert deliberately or otherwise misinterpreted it when using it as a justification to fight at Marston Moor. But in fact, making due allowance for the King's customary convoluted style, and his evident desire not to ruffle the prince's delicate sensibilities, it is clear that, unless shortage of powder prevented it, Rupert was instructed both to relieve York and defeat the Allied armies. Indeed it would not be possible permanently to raise the siege without such a victory, partic-ularly if the prince and his army were then intended to march south to join the King without delay.

With the benefit of hindsight, Lord Clarendon later wrote:[29]

Lord Culpeper [one of the King's Privy Council] not present at the writing of the letter or the consultation, as I suppose, but coming in after, asked the

King 'If the letter was sent?', who said 'yes' – 'Why then,' says he, 'before God you are undone, for upon this peremptory order he will fight, whatever comes on't.

Whether anything of the sort was actually said is no longer provable, but in any case Rupert regarded the instruction as a binding one. He is said to have carried the letter – as his justification – about with him for the rest of his life.[30]

The die was now cast; Rupert ended the discussion with Newcastle by saying:[31] 'Nothing venture, nothing have' He still evidently hoped to attack that day, but as the hours stretched into early afternoon, still with no sign of the York foot, and the Allied armies steadily forming up on the ridge opposite his position, the Royalist opportunity was fast slipping away.

5

MARSTON MOOR: PRELUDE TO BATTLE, AFTERNOON 2 JULY

The terrain over which the opposing armies were in process of deploying formed two sharply contrasting areas. To the south, running roughly from east to west, was the ridge on which the Allied cavalry had been stationed for much of the morning. It reached its greatest height (38 metres) at the distinctive point later known as Cromwell's Clump. From here the ridge descends in a northerly direction to 15 metres over a distance of 1440 metres. The drop is initially quite steep, to 30 metres in 70 metres, into a hollow, followed by a slight rise, then more gradual descent for another 275 metres to the 23-metre line, roughly along which much of the Allied army was initially deployed. The fall is then much more gradual to the line occupied by the Royalist forces: by the evening after initial adjustments about 350 metres from their opponents.

In July 1644 the ridge and the slopes on its northern side were under cultivation, apparently forming one large open field of corn or rye. The field extended northwards to the track running between the villages of Long Marston and Tockwith, half a mile north of Cromwell's Clump, and perhaps a further 350 metres northwards to the edge of the moorland.

Marston Moor itself, where the Royalists deployed, was a vast, virtually flat area, covered with a mixture of scrub, grass and gorse, with a few thorn bushes, and some noticeably boggy areas, particularly at its eastern end near Tockwith. The moor was crossed by a number of roughly cobbled tracks, used by cattle drovers, several of which met at the junction known as Four Lanes Meet, in the vicinity of which, and on the fringes of the two villages, there may have been a few small fields. On the northwestern edge of the moor lay Wilstrop Wood, mainly oak and elm, and probably somewhat greater in extent than is the case today.[1]

Three principal routes led on to Marston Moor. The northernmost was the road to Boroughbridge, used by Rupert's army on the morning of 2 July. Leading directly from York's Micklegate to the village of Hessay on the northeastern fringe of the moor, and then on to the moor itself, was a cobbled road. This was the route taken by Newcastle's laggard infantry and by the marquis himself. The third route led southwards over the ridge in the direction of Wetherby, and was the one along which the Allied foot were marching in the morning prior to their recall.

There were two other significant tracks. One from the south crossed the ridge at a point later known as Cromwell's Gap, and crossed the Tockwith–Long Marston road about 200 yards west of Long Marston. From here, known today as Atterwith Lane, it ran northwards through a strip of cultivated land near the village, and then on across the moor, eventually joining the Boroughbridge road.. The other track of significance in the battle is now known as Moor Lane, and after running north from the Tockwith–Long Marston road for about half a mile, divides at Four Lanes Meet. The eastern branch became the Hessay–York road, the northern branch eventually joined the Boroughbridge road, and the western one swung northwest around Wilstrop Wood in the direction of the River Nidd.

Much debate has centred around the exact nature of the hedge and ditch usually said to have marked the boundary between the cultivated lands and Marston Moor itself. Inspired in part by the representation in Bernard De Gomme's plan of the Royalist deployment,[2] it is sometimes suggested that the hedge and ditch presented a continuous and fairly significant barrier. In fact, it is clear from accounts of the fighting that although there was a hedge and ditch of sorts, not necessarily very substantial, between the opposing foot in the centre, on the Allied left it was almost entirely non-existent.

The barrier was most substantial on the Allied right and possibly right centre. This was especially noticable in the area of Atterwith Lane, where there was evidently a steep bank, possibly topped by a hedge, which may have dropped as much as 6ft down to the moor. The bank was breached only at the point where it was crossed by Atterwith Lane.

The feature continued for perhaps 150 yards westwards from Atterwith Lane, mostly as a fairly shallow ditch with a hedge on its northern side, but at some point it seems to have faded out almost entirely.

The other main topographical features which influenced the battle were to be found in the area of the Allied left wing. Most striking was a large artificial rabbit warren known as Bilton Bream, situated on rising ground, which was the centre of skirmishing during the morning, and which Parliamentarian pioneers probably had to partially level in order to clear a passage for their cavalry.

The Royalist right wing was deployed behind a 'cross ditch or drain', not a continuation of the hedge and ditch boundary discussed above, but possibly intended to drain some boggy ground in the vicinity and forming the boundary between the parishes of Long Marston and Tockwith. After initially running southwards, the ditch angles southwest for 200 yards, separating the Royalist position from Bilton Bream.[3]

38. Harquebusiers as depicted in John Cruso, *Militarie Instructions for the Cavallerie*, 1635.
These troops are well equipped with carbine, pair of pistols and sword,
and wear back and breast plates and 'pot' helmets.

Before examining the deployment of the opposing forces and the final hours before battle, it is worth looking briefly at some of the main features of the armies of 1644.

Cavalry – 'the horse' – were traditionally the elite, battle-winning arm. Military writers recommended that an army should have a horse/foot ratio of 1:2. In practice, however, various factors, notably the much higher rate of desertion among the foot, which contained many more conscripts than the cavalry, meant that these proportions were sometimes almost reversed, or at best roughly equal. The latter was approximately the situation among Prince Rupert's forces at Marston Moor.

There were three recognised types of cavalry.[4] Rarely employed in the English Civil War was the heavy horseman or cuirassier, with three-quarter length armour and a heavy charger. The latter were difficult to obtain and maintain, and the armour was uncomfortable and expensive, so that by 1644 few except some senior officers were so equipped.

Lancers, still widely used on the Continent, were not a feature of the English armies, though they remained popular with the Scots, being seen as a compensation for the relatively light horses available to the Scottish cavalry. Each cavalry regiment had a troop of lancers attached, and they could on occasion be quite effective, especially against infantry.[5]

The standard cavalryman of 1644 was the 'harquebusier'. Technically classed as light cavalry, they were generally equipped with 'pot' helmet, back and breast plates, and armed with sword, pair of pistols and sometimes a carbine or short-barrelled musket, which had replaced the 'harquebus' from which their name was derived.[6] By 1644 both sides employed them in the 'shock' role originally performed by the cuirassier.

Cavalry regiments in the Royalist and Parliamentarian armies theoretically totalled about 500 men, though in practice numbers varied enormously. Many regiments on both sides at Marston Moor were considerably weaker, in some cases 'brigaded' together to form viable units. On the other hand, Cromwell's own regiment of horse, his celebrated 'Ironsides', was a 'double-regiment' of 800 or more men. The basic tactical unit was the 'troop', consisting of four officers (captain, lieutenant, cornet and quartermaster), two trumpeters and sixty men. The number per regiment varied widely from two or three in a weak unit, up to ten in a full-strength formation. It was customary in battle to brigade troops together into 'divisions' of about 500 men.

Although the proportion is often considerably exaggerated, Royalist cavalry regiments probably contained a marginally higher number of men of 'gentry' origin than did their Parliamentarian counterparts. But the majority of troopers on both sides were tradesmen, husbandmen, grooms and other outdoor servants with a fair number of townsmen as well. Newcastle's Northern Horse were perhaps unique in including a woman officer, the remarkable Capt. Frances Dalyell, an illegitimate

39. A pikeman. This figure is unusual in wearing morion-style helmet, back and breast plates and tassets protecting his thighs. Few pikemen at Marston Moor are likely to have worn any armour, except perhaps for a headpiece.

daughter of the Scottish Earl of Carnwath, who rode under a standard ominously depicting a hanged man.[7]

A foot regiment had an again largely theoretical establishment of 1,200 men organised in ten companies of varying size. Military doctrine recommended a 1:2 pike/musket ratio, but this also varied widely. When sufficient firearms were available, the proportion of musketeers was often higher, with an increasing number of all-musketeer regiments, though it is uncertain whether any of the latter were present at Marston Moor. It was common practice to detach parties of musketeers from individual regiments to form 'commanded' bodies, varying in size from fifty to 1,000 men, either to act as skirmishers, to provide firepower support for cavalry, or for other special purposes.[8]

The pike was theoretically a 16ft-long weapon, though for ease of use it was often shortened to about 12ft. Pikemen had originally worn body armour, but this fell into disuse virtually from the start of the war, and other than some pot or 'morion' style helmets, probably little if any was worn by troops at Marston Moor.[9] When involved in combat with their enemy opposite numbers, pikemen engaged in the tactic known as 'push of pike'. This procedure (not unlike a modern rugby scrum) was designed to disorganise enemy ranks, knock opponents off their feet and push them back. In practice, particularly if both sides were poorly motivated or unenthusiastic, contests often degenerated into deadlocked 'fencing matches', with ineffectually clashing pikes. Unless one opponent broke and attempted to flee, casualties were usually light.

The other major role of the pikemen lay in fending off cavalry attacks. Musketeers sheltered under the protection of a 'hedgehog' formed by the pikes, and attempted to repel cavalry by their fire or clubbed musket.

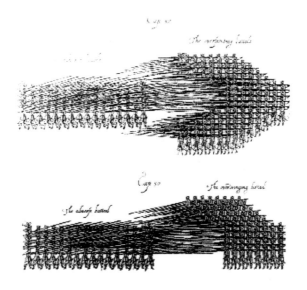

40. 'Push of pike'. The formation on the right in the upper illustration is attempting to attack the unprotected flanks of its opponents. (John Bingham, *Tactiks of Aelian*, 1616).

The musketeer's standard weapon was the matchlock musket. This weapon was cheap to produce and simple to use, though it was often ineffective in damp conditions. Although it had a theoretical range of 400 yards, it was only really effective at 100 yards or less. Contemporary drill books contain complicated loading and firing procedures, which have caused many writers seriously to underestimate the possible rate of fire. The greatly simplified drill normally used in combat situations meant however that a reasonably competent musketeer could fire every 30 seconds.

Most infantry combats, if pressed home, and assuming that the opposing side did not flee or retreat, eventually became hand-to-hand contests. In these the musketeer preferred to use his musket-butt, rather than the cheap and usually ineffective sword with which he was also equipped.

Musketeers were normally deployed in six ranks, each firing in succession, then wheeling to the rear to reload. By this means a well-trained unit could keep up virtually continuous fire. It was also possible to fire a 'salvo' or 'salvee' by three ranks at once, which could be highly effective, with the penalty of the subsequent loss of firepower whilst the musketeers reloaded.

Exchanges of musket fire could be quite prolonged, particularly if troops were reluctant to close with their opponents, but, like 'push of pike', were not generally

41. Seventeenth-century dragoons. Despite what this illustration suggests, dragoons normally dismounted to fire.

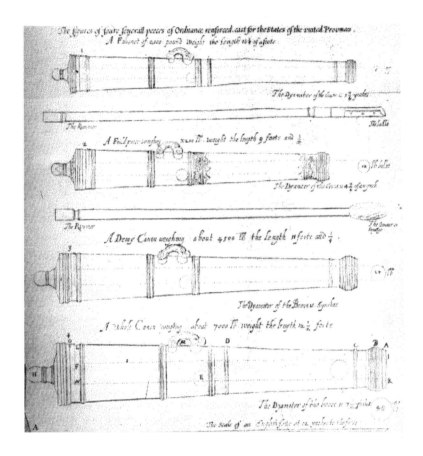

42. Contemporary illustration of various kinds of artillery. A six-pounder is at the top, followed by a demi-culverin, demi-cannon and full cannon.

very deadly in their effects. Most casualties were inflicted when troops routed, especially if they were pursued by cavalry.

Dragoons, of whom a significant number were present at Marston Moor, were basically mounted infantry. They were normally armed with a short-barrelled musket or firelock, and usually fought dismounted in the role of skirmishers. They were often employed to clear hedges or other enemy strongpoints, and push back outlying defenders.

The Royalists by 1644 had few full regiments of dragoons (only one, Henry Washington's, was probably at Marston Moor) but some cavalry regiments, particularly those of Newcastle's Northern Horse, included a troop of dragoons in their establishment. The Allies had two English and one Scots dragoon regiments, which again theoretically averaged 500–600 men each.

Artillery tended to play a limited role in battle, its main value being in siege operations. However there were occasions, as for example at the First Battle of Newbury, when cannon fire inflicted significant losses. Although both sides used artillery at Marston Moor, there is no evidence to suggest that it had any major effect. It is unlikely that either side deployed their heaviest guns (whole cannon of about 63lb, and slightly lighter demi-cannon and culverin, which were primarily siege pieces) but both evidently made use of medium-rated demi-culverin and lighter pieces, which went under a variety of names, such as drakes, sakers and falcons, which generally fired 3lb shot or less. The Scots also had over eighty of their light 'frame' guns, which were intended for anti-personnel use.

When examining the deployment of the opposing armies at Marston Moor, we are reliant largely on contemporary sources, including plans. The latter at first sight appear to answer most of the questions posed, but it is worth examining the circumstances in which they were compiled, and their consequent limitations.

Before the start of a campaign, a seventeenth-century commander would discuss with his senior officers his ideal plan for the deployment of his army in battle. Normally this would draw heavily on contemporary military theory and particularly admired examples dating as far back as classical times. The result would be drawn up on paper as a 'headquarters plan'.[10] Copies of the plan would be given to subordinate commanders down to brigade level, with overall responsibility for its implementation resting with the sergeant major general of the army. If possible, the deployment would be practised beforehand.

In practice, of course, the original plan would often be significantly altered by the terrain or circumstances in which a battle was eventually fought, the addition of reinforcements or the absence of troops available when the plan was first drawn up.

Prince Rupert's engineer-general, Sir Bernard De Gomme, in the post-Restoration period, produced finely drawn copies of the original battle plans for four of the engagements in which the prince was involved during the Civil War. His plan of Marston Moor[11] provides a detailed record of the intended deployment of the troops brought to the field by Prince Rupert. It does not however give more than an approximation, probably based on additions hastily drawn in at the time, of the composition and deployment of many of Newcastle's troops, particularly his foot. There is also evidence that a few other units, such as the Royalist dragoons, were omitted, and some of the actual deployments in the field, even of Rupert's contingent of the army, may have varied from those planned. With these provisos, however, De Gomme's plan must be our main source for the deployment of the Royalist forces.

The Royalist army occupied a frontage of about $1\frac{1}{2}$ miles, almost exactly filling the interval between the villages of Tockwith and Long Marston. The line of the ditch and hedge, about 100 yards in front of the main position, was probably occupied by several hundred 'commanded' musketeers and dismounted dragoons, supported by at least four light guns or drakes. Their task would be to disrupt and hopefully delay an advancing enemy, and then fall back on their main force.

The Royalist right wing consisted of 2,600 horse, supported by 500 musketeers, (possibly Washington's dragoons) in two lines. It was commanded by Lord John Byron, with Sgt-Maj.-Gen. Sir John Urry as his second-in-command. Urry was a reasonably competent Scottish professional soldier, who had made the first of three

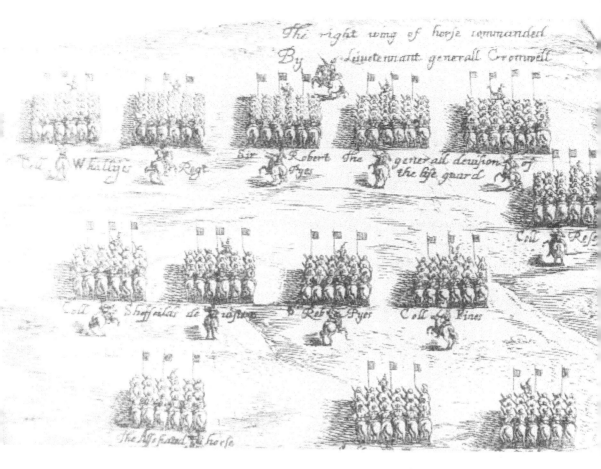

43. Detail from Edward Streeter's 'Plan of the Battle of Naseby', showing cavalry deployment.
Regiments are formed into squadrons, generally about 250 strong. Squadrons are deployed
in 'chequerboard' formation for mutual support. Note the formation deployed between
the first and second lines, 'refusing' (protecting) the right flank.

changes of allegiance in June 1643, when he had quit the service of the Earl of Essex
in order to join the Royalists. Rupert evidently rated him quite highly, though on
exactly what grounds is unclear. Byron was a highly effective cavalry commander, but
his actual standing on the day is uncertain. Rupert had not apparently appointed a
general or lieutenant-general of horse in his army, and Byron appears still to have
held his old rank of field marshal-general (approximating to second-in-command of
Rupert's army). It may be that his command of the right wing was seen as temporary,
with Rupert intending, as he would a year later at Naseby, to assume personal control
once battle began.

It seems likely that Urry commanded Byron's first line, which consisted of four
regiments, totalling 1,100 horse. To the right rear of Byron's first line was stationed
Sir Samuel Tuke's regiment of horse, about 200 strong. It was technically 'refusing'
the flank, that is, offering some protection against an attack on the Royalist right

flank in the absence of any natural feature to secure it. Slightly to the left of the front line were the 400 men of Marcus Trevor's regiment of horse, possibly intended to give some cover to the right flank of the Royalist foot at a point where the ditch offered little, if any, protection.

Byron's second line, commanded by Richard, Lord Molyneux, an experienced cavalry officer from Lancashire who had served in the Oxford Army, consisted of 800 men, including his own and Sir Thomas Tyldesley's regiments, both experienced units. Slightly to their left, stationed where they could move forward into the interval between the main part of Byron's front line and Trevor's regiment, or against the right flank of any attackers, was Prince Rupert's redoubtable regiment of horse – at 500 men, probably the strongest cavalry unit in the Royalist army.

The command structure of the 11,000 or so foot forming the Royalist centre is unclear. It seems to have been intended that Lord Eythin should take overall command, with Tillier and Sir Francis Mackworth leading Rupert and Newcastle's contingents respectively.

The foot apparently formed twenty-two divisions, each about 500 strong. The most puzzling feature of De Gomme's plan is its depiction of a body of foot, consisting of Prince Rupert's and Lord Byron's regiments, possibly up to 1,500 men in all, deployed to the right front of Trevor's regiment. This is almost certainly a late alteration to the original battle plan, intended perhaps to give additional protection to the vulnerable area on Byron's left.

The first line of Royalist foot formed eight bodies, of perhaps 4,000 men. These consisted of six regiments of Rupert's army, including five of the units from Ireland. In April the regiments of Warren, Erneley and Gibson, all mauled at Nantwich, had totalled 1,000 men, and, as Erneley and Gibson were brigaded together, were probably no stronger now. Also in the first line were Henry Tillier and Robert Broughton's regiments, each at least 500 men, and Sir Thomas Tyldesley's recently raised Lancashire foot regiment.

The composition of the second line is less certain. For much of the morning it must have been thinly spread, consisting of perhaps 1,800 men of Henry Cheater's Cumbrian foot, the Derbyshire troops under John Milward and another newly raised Lancashire regiment led by Edward Chisenall. In the course of the afternoon these were shuffled to the left as their place on the right was filled by three divisions of northern foot. These probably consisted of a number of weak regiments, brigaded together in divisions of 500 each.

Newcastle's remaining foot, about 1,500 men, probably including his own regiment, originally possibly a 'double' regiment and hence still probably more than 500 men, were, according to the evidence of De Gomme's Plan, intended to form a third supporting line. However it is fairly certain that they were still filing on to the moor, in the vicinity of Four Lanes Meet, when fighting began.

For much of the day, Rupert's main concern must have been the weakness of his centre. In an attempt to support it, and also in line with contemporary Continental practice, he backed his second line of foot with a brigade of about 800 northern cavalry under Sir William Blakiston.

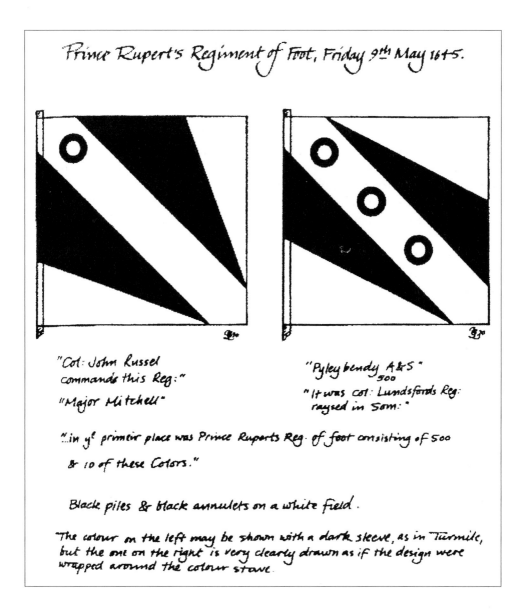

Prince Rupert's Regiment of Foot, Friday 9th May 1645.

"Col: John Russel
commands this Reg:"

"Major Mitchell"

"Pyley bendy A&S"
500

"It was col: Lundsfords Reg:
raysed in Som:"

"...in ye primeir place was Prince Ruperts Reg. of foot consisting of 500
& 10 of these Colors."

Black piles & black annulets on a white field.

The colour on the left may be shown with a dark sleeve, as in Turmile,
but the one on the right is very clearly drawn as if the design were
wrapped around the colour stave.

44. Possible reconstruction of the flags carried during part of the war
by Prince Rupert's regiment of foot. Their design is unusual, not following
any of the more commonly used systems, though as with other examples,
the number of amulets on each flag denotes the seniority of the officer it represents,
first and third captains being depicted here.

In reserve just south of the present-day White Syke Close, Rupert had a small formation consisting of his lifeguard of horse (150 men) and the 400 northern troopers of Lord Widdrington's brigade. It was a inadequate force to have any impact, and it may be that the prince had intended the latecomers of Newcastle's foot also to form part of the reserve.

The Royalist left wing totalled 2,100 horse, supported by at least 500 musketeers, under Lord George Goring. Despite his later reputation as an unprincipled intriguer and libertine, Goring was a highly capable cavalry commander, arguably the best in the Royalist armies next to Rupert himself. There are grounds to believe that De Gomme is not entirely accurate in his depiction of the deployment of Goring's wing, and some of the details remain uncertain.

The first line probably consisted of about 1,100 troopers, including a brigade of northern horse about 800 strong, possibly that commanded by Sir Richard Dacre, with some Derbyshire and Newark horse, commanded either by Rowland Eyre or conceivably Sir John Mayney.[12] 'Refusing' the flank in the same way as Samuel Tuke on Byron's wing was Sir Francis Carnaby, with perhaps 200 men.

Goring himself appears to have led his first line. The second, commanded by Sir Charles Lucas, included his own and Sir Marmaduke Langdale's brigades, about 800 men in total.

In all the Royalist army probably consisted of at least 4,500 horse and 12,000 to 13,000 foot and dragoons. Rupert's heavy guns had been left in York, but he had a number of medium and lighter pieces with him from his own artillery train. There is no evidence that Newcastle contributed any artillery.

The Allied deployment was based in part on a rough battle plan drawn up by Leven's major-general, Sir James Lumsden, but it was in general more improvised than that of their opponents. The horse on the wings occupied more or less their pre-determined positions, but the foot in the centre were probably deployed to a large extent more or less in the order in which they returned from the Tadcaster march, starting with the Eastern Association forces (which had been at the rear of the column) on the left, and with the Allied armies more intermingled than would have been preferred.

The right wing, commanded by Sir Thomas Fairfax, consisted of about 3,000 horse, forming three lines. The first, under Fairfax's personal command, totalled about 1,000 men, a mix of his veteran units and some new levied troops. The second line, of similar strength, under Col. John Lambert, was formed from other units of Lord Fairfax's army. In reserve was a third line of 1,000 troopers consisting of three Scottish regiments under the Earl of Eglinton. Fairfax was supported by 500 dragoons, probably the northern regiment of Col. Thomas Morgan, and 600 'commanded' musketeers.[13]

Despite the survival of Lumley's fragmentary battle plan,[14] some uncertainty remains regarding the details of the deployment of the Allied foot, totalling up to 20,000 men, in the centre, and also regarding their exact command structure. The Earl of Leven was with the foot, who in the case of the Scots were under the operational command of major-generals William Baillie and Sir James Lumsden. It seems that Lord Fairfax probably commanded the foot of his army in person. Command of

45. George, Lord Goring (1608–57). As a wild young man, Goring served with the Dutch until wounded in the ankle at the Siege of Breda (1637), and lamed for life. He served in the Scots Wars, after which he became enmeshed in an intrigue which in 1642 found him Parliament's governor of Portsmouth. Changing sides he fled to Holland, returning in late 1642 as Newcastle's general of horse. He defeated Sir Thomas Fairfax at Seacroft Moor (March 1643), but was imprisoned for nine months after being captured in May at Wakefield. After Marston Moor Goring became lieutenant-general of horse in the Oxford Army, where his considerable military abilities were gradually clouded by illness, dissipation, and his insatiable love of intrigue.

46. Col. Thomas Morgan (d.1679?). A diminutive Welshman, who after serving
in the Low Countries, commanded dragoons in the Northern Parliamentarian forces.
He was later a major-general.

the Eastern Association foot was probably divided, with Maj.-Gen. Lawrence
Crawford leading the bulk of the units which were stationed on the left, whilst the
Earl of Manchester commanded a brigade, which probably included his own
regiment, at the right of the third line.

The Allied foot seem to have been organised into fourteen brigades, in the case of
the Scots each consisting of two regiments. These were apparently brigaded so far as
possible with the aim of having men from neighbouring localities serving together.
The strength of the Eastern Association infantry can be determined from muster rolls
as being in the region of 4,500 men.[15] But totals for the other contingents are more
problematic. The Scots had certainly suffered considerable wastage of various kinds
since January, and they may have been as few as 11,000 men at Marston Moor.[16] It
seems unlikely, even allowing for some reinforcements from Lancashire, that Lord
Fairfax can have had more than 4,000 foot.

The Allied foot were deployed in four lines. The first line, of about 7,500 men,
was formed into five brigades. On the left were two brigades of Eastern Association
foot, under Lawrence Crawford. To their right, in the centre of the line, was a
brigade of Lord Fairfax's army, probably under their general's own command. The
right of the first line was formed by two Scots brigades under Lt-Gen. Baillie.

The second line consisted of four Scots brigades, or about 6,000 men,
commanded by Maj.-Gen. Sir James Lumsden. The third line, of similar strength,

again included four brigades. On the left were two from Lord Fairfax's army, with a Scots brigade to their right and beyond that an Eastern Association brigade, probably formed by the Earl of Manchester's strong regiment of foot under his own command. To the rear was a further brigade, probably Scots.

The Allied left totalled approximately 4,000 horse, and 500–1,000 dragoons, some deployed in support of the horse, under Lt-Gen. Oliver Cromwell of the Army of the Eastern Association. They were deployed in three lines, the first consisting of five divisions of Eastern Association cavalry, about 1,500 troopers in all, including Cromwell's own regiment, and under his personal command. The second line, another five divisions each of about 300 men, were also Eastern Association horse, probably commanded by their commissary-general, Bartholomew Vermuyden. To their rear was a third line formed from 1,000 Scots horse led by Lt-Gen. David Leslie, who probably acted as Cromwell's second-in-command.

Also with Cromwell's wing, and destined to play a key role in coming events, was the 500-strong Scots dragoon regiment of Col. Hugh Frazer, which seems to have been deployed on Cromwell's left flank.

Most of the Allied artillery was probably deployed on the higher ground of the ridge to the rear of the army, but Cromwell had at least two light guns with his wing,

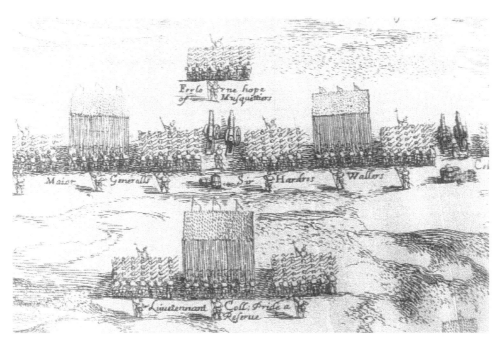

47. Foot deployed for battle in Streeter's 'Plan of the Battle Naseby'. At the top is a block of musketeers acting as a 'forlorn hope'. The main infantry force is deployed in blocks, each of around 500 men, each body of pikes being flanked by musketeers. Light guns are stationed in the intervals between divisions, which are themselves in 'chequerboard' formation, so that units in the second line can move up into the intervals of the first. Note the officers (normally lieutenants) stationed behind each division to regulate its formation and prevent desertions.

48. Edward Montagu, 2nd Earl of Manchester (1602–71). 'A sweet meek man', according to Robert Baillie, Manchester became a supporter of the Puritan faction in Parliament perhaps more as a result of pressure from his wife than out of deeply held conviction. On 19 August 1643 he became major-general of the Army of the Eastern Association. Manchester was a capable administrator with concern for the welfare of his men, but was an uninspired soldier. He would become increasingly disillusioned after Marston Moor by the growing influence of the radicals, including Cromwell, in Parliament.

and it seems likely that the Scots had their light frame guns stationed with their brigades of foot.

The Allied commanders spent some tense hours as their foot gradually returned to the ridge and took up position. They remained vulnerable to attack until about 2 p.m., when[17] 'we had indifferently well formed our army'. The right wing of the Royalist army was 'drawne up within shot of our ordnance',[18] and at about 2 p.m. the Parliamentarian artillery commenced a desultory bombardment, to which Royalist guns replied. Firing, possibly hindered by 'some showers of rain' which may have affected the powder, continued at intervals for up to three hours. Little real damage seems to have been inflicted by either side, except that the Royalist right was forced[19] 'to leave that ground and remove to a greater distance'. It may have been at this point that they pulled further back from the higher ground, crossed by the Long Marston–Tockwith road, facing Bilton Bream.

Whilst the cannonade continued, acrimonious debate went on among the Royalist high command. It was about 4 p.m. or later that Eythin eventually put in an appear-

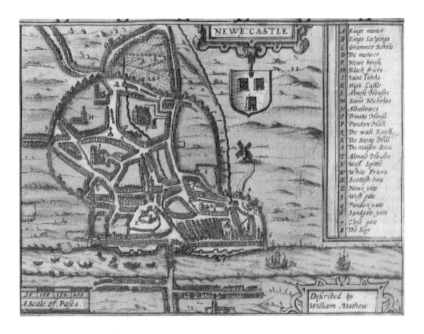

1. John Speed's map of Newcastle-on-Tyne, c.1611.
Note the extent of the medieval walls and the dock facilities.

2. John Speed's map of York, c.1611. The suburbs have extended for some distance
beyond the original medieval defences. Note the additional protection provided by rivers,
and the large number of windmills in the vicinity of the city.

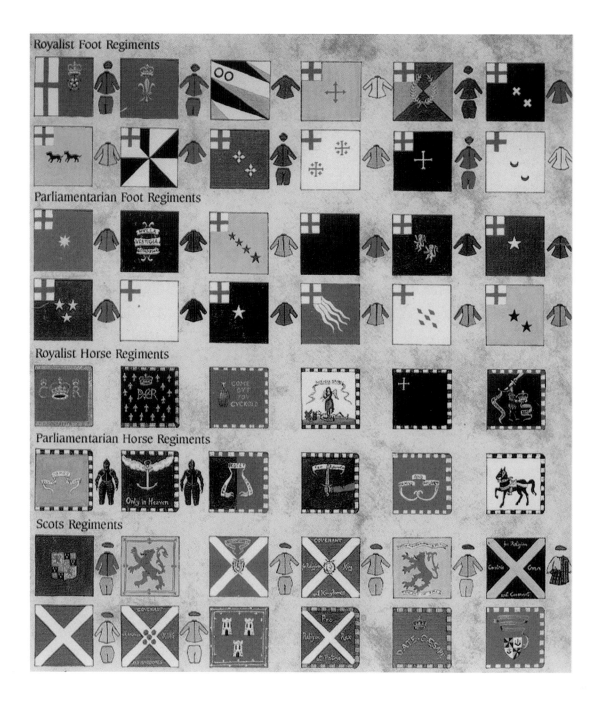

3. A selection of the flags carried by units in the Civil War. In the case of infantry colours,
the number and arrangement of devices on the flag fields were often indicative of the rank of officer
with whom it was associated. Cavalry cornets often bore a political or religious slogan or cartoon.

4. Ensign, Army of the Solemn League and Covenant. This soldier,
with his 'hodden grey' breeches and blue bonnet, is typical of the appearance
of the Earl of Leven's soldiers. As an officer, he is fortunate to have acquired a buff coat.
Many, though not all, Scots foot colours included the Cross of St Andrew in their design.

5. Musketeers in action. These soldiers could be either Royalist or Parliamentarian,
though the wounded officer, judging by his crimson sash, is a Cavalier. Note the variety
of headgear, including felt hats and 'montero' caps. They are deployed in three ranks,
the first firing, the second at the 'ready' and the third loading.

6. St Mary's Tower and adjoining section of city walls, York,
which saw intensive fighting during the attempt by the Eastern Association foot
under Lawrence Crawford to storm the defences on 17 June.

7. Section of city walls near St Mary's Tower,
showing evidence of damage suffered during the siege.

8. Looking south from the crest of the 'lower slope' towards the upper ridge line. 'Cromwell's Clump' is upper left. The hollow area between the two ridges, possibly initially used to conceal the Allied third line, and where broken Royalist cavalry massed towards the end of the battle, is clearly visible

9. View looking south from the Long Marston-Tockwith road towards the centre of the intial Allied position. 'Cromwell's Clump' is visible (centre-left). The first line of Allied foot was probably deployed just forward of the crest of the 'lower slope' occupied here by ploughed land

10. Looking north from the crest of the lower ridge, following the slope down which the Allied foot advanced. The main Royalist position lay along the line of the hedgerow (centre left). Moor Lane is visible to the right of the monument, with the line of hedges around Four Lanes Meet and extending to White Syke Close (left), in the area where the Royalist reserve and the late-arriving Northern foot were positioned at the start of the battle, visible in the background. Wilstrop Wood lies on the horizon (left).

11. View south from Long Marston-Tockwith road towards 'Cromwell's Clump' marked by a clump of trees on horizon. Allied foot were deployed on the slope forward of this point, with Fairfax's cavalry roughly around the area marked by the diagonally sloping hedge (upper left). The Allied baggage train was probably just beyond the crest of the ridge in the same area.

12. Centre of the Royalist position, seen from the Long Marston–Tockwith road.
The forward line of Royalist musketeers was stationed along the line
of the hedgerow in the background.

13. Bilton Bream area, looking westwards from the lower slope of the ridge .
It was across this area that Cromwell's cavalry advanced at the start of the battle.
The rising ground crossed by the Long Marston-Tockwith road (right) may be the area
from which the Royalists were driven in skirmishing on the morning of 2 July.

14. View towards position occupied by Byron's horse at the start of the battle.
The brigade of foot formed by Rupert and Byron's regiments was probably positioned
along the hedgerow (centre right).

15. Slope down which Cromwell's cavalry advanced from Bilton Bream.

16. Looking northwards from the lower slope of Marston Ridge towards the position (centre right) occupied by Goring's horse at the start of the battle.

17. View from Atterwith Lane, from the approximate position of Goring's front line, looking southwards towards Long Marston. Fairfax advanced along and to the right of the lane.

18. Looking westwards from the centre of the Allied start line towards Tockwith,
and the area of the cavalry engagement between Cromwell and Byron.
Wilstrop Wood can be seen centre right.

19. Near Goring's position on Atterwith Lane the remains of the hedge and steep bank which
separated Marston Moor from the cultivated land to the south can still clearly be seen.

20. Looking westwards from Atterwith Lane over the area where the engagement between Lambert and Goring's force took place. The final encounter between Cromwell and the Northern horse may have been in the same approximate area.

21. Four Lanes Meet. It was probably in its immediate vicinity that Newcastle was resting in his coach at the commencement of the battle.

22. Looking south along Moor Lane from the Royalist position towards Marston Ridge. 'Cromwell's Clump' may be seen on the horizon, with the monument (centre).

23. Looking northeastwards from Four Lanes Meet along the old Hessay Road along which Newcastle and his foot marched from York on 2 July, and which formed the line of retreat of many Royalist fugitives at the end of the battle.

24. View south from near White Syke Close towards the Royalist front line,
along hedgerow (centre right). It was near this point that Rupert and the Royalist reserve
were stationed at the start of the battle.

25. Looking northwards from White Syke Close towards Wilstrop Wood.
Many of Byron's broken horse fled across the intervening open ground, which also
saw the advance of part of Cromwell's cavalry moving eastwards to engage Goring.

26. View northwestwards from Moor Lane towards White Syke Close.
This area, with Four Lane Meet at the upper right, saw bitter fighting in the closing stages
of the battle. It was probably here that the 'last stand' of the Whitecoats took place.

27. White Syke Close. Although the trees post-date the battle,
the site is traditionally identified with the 'last stand' of Newcastle's Whitecoats.
One of the mass grave pits of those who died in the battle is nearby.

28. 'Cromwell after Marston Moor' by Ernest Crofts. As Cromwell and his weary troopers
drew rein after routing Goring's horse on the evening of 2 July 1644, they had played
a decisive role in winning Parliament's greatest victory of the war so far.
Cromwell had taken a major step on his road to greatness.

ance at the head of a straggling column of northern foot from York. Initially there may have been as few as 2,500 men, with others, possibly including Newcastle's regiment of foot, still on the road, and according to Rupert's *Diary*,[20] 'all drunk'. A tense encounter followed between Rupert and Eythin: —[21]

> The Prince demanded of King [Eythin] how he liked the marshalling of his army, who replied that he did not approve of it being drawn too near the enemy, and in a place of disadvantage, then said the Prince 'they may be drawn to a further distance.' 'No sir,' said King, 'it is too late.' It is so, King dissuaded the prince from fighting, saying, 'Sir, your forwardness cost us the day in Germany, where yourself was taken prisoner': upon the dissuasions of the Marquis and King and that it was so near night, the Prince was resolved not to join battle that day, and therefore gave order to have provisions for his army brought from York.

In another version of the exchange:[22]

> When Major-General King came up Prince Rupert showed the Marquis and the Earl a paper, which he said was the draught of the battle as he meant to fight it, and asked them what they thought of it. King answered: 'By God, sir, it is very fine in the paper, but there is no such thing in the fields.' The Prince replied 'Not so', etc. The Marquis asked the Prince what he would do? His Highness answered 'We will charge them tomorrow morning.' My Lord asked him, whether he was sure the enemy would not fall on them sooner; he answered 'No!'

Rupert told Newcastle:[23]

> ...to repose himself till then. Which My Lord did, and went to rest in his own coach that was close by in the field [probably in the vicinity of Four Lanes Meet], until the time appointed.

Rupert himself retired to eat supper with his lifeguard stationed with the reserve. His senior commanders probably settled down to eat in the vicinity of their troops, which remained in formation, in the case of the cavalry with saddled horses, bridles in hand, but there was apparently a general stand-down and slackening of alertness.

Of all Rupert's errors in the run-up to battle, his certainty that the enemy would not attack that day was the most serious. There were at least three hours of daylight remaining, and the Allies had shortly beforehand made a general advance some 200 yards closer to the Royalist position. For the moment they seemed content to remain in line, singing psalms,[24] but the assumption that they would remain inactive for the evening was a dangerous one. It may well be that the explanation lies in the fraught relationship between the prince, Newcastle and Eythin. Rupert seems to have achieved the not inconsiderable feat of keeping his stormy temper more or less under control during his highly frustrating exchanges with his Northern Army colleagues, but he must now have been approaching the end of his tether. He may simply have felt unable to argue with them any longer, and cut short the discussions, convincing himself that nothing would happen that day, and, significantly perhaps, choosing not to eat with Newcastle.

The extent of his miscalculation was about to become apparent.

6

MARSTON MOOR:
PHASE ONE, 7 P.M.–8.30 P.M.

As the Royalists, with the probable exception of their forward line of musketeers, broke ranks in anticipation of their evening meal, no such relaxation was apparent among their opponents. Though the area of dead ground between the rear and forward ridges possibly hid the Allied third line from Royalist sight, and gave a false impression of enemy strength and preparedness, the Allies, who at some stage had advanced a further 200 yards towards the Royalist position, remained formed up.

Amongst most of them there was not, however, any real expectation of imminent action. Manchester's scoutmaster-general, Lionel Watson, wrote:[1]

> In this posture we stood until seven of the clock, so that it was concluded on our side that there would be no ingagement that night, neither of the two Armies agreeing to begin the charge…

At about the same time that the Royalists stood down, Leven and the other Allied generals were surveying their position from the high ground, probably from the point now known as 'Cromwell's Clump'. Something which they observed made the normally cautious Leven and his equally unadventurous fellow-generals resolve to stake everything on a general attack. Given that neither Manchester nor Lord Fairfax were noted as rapid decision-makers, it seems likely that the moving spirits were their more dynamic subordinates – Cromwell, Crawford and Sir Thomas Fairfax. Contemporary accounts are generally uninformative as to their reasoning, so we can only speculate on why the decision was reached. It would certainly already have been apparent to the Allied leaders that they had a significant numerical advantage, assisted by the Royalist decision to stand down. Possibly more significant was the sight of the last of the northern foot in the process of deploying on to the field. They were probably still in the vicinity of Four Lanes Meet, so that the Royalist third line was as yet incomplete, and perhaps in the process of 'shuffling' to the right in order to accom-

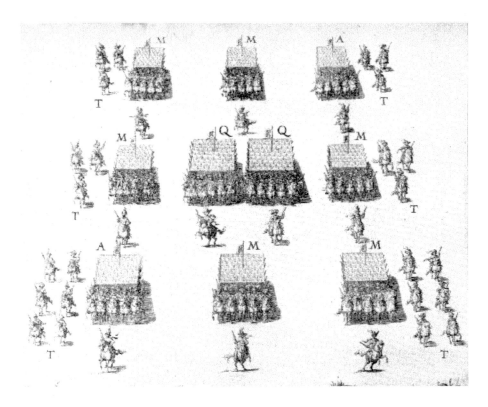

49. A less common cavalry deployment, with mounted dragoons on the flanks.

modate the latecomers. The Royalist Arthur Trevor, though not himself present at this stage, appeared to hint at as much when he wrote:[2] 'The enemy perceiving the advance of that addition to the Prince's army instantly charged our horse.'

Estimates of the time at which the Allied advance began vary widely from about 6 p.m. to as much as two hours later. Most probably it was between 7 p.m. and 7.30 p.m. when, signalled by a discharge of Allied guns, though probably not by the peals of thunder mentioned in many secondary accounts, the attack began.

Watson, with Cromwell on the Allied left, remembered:[3]

About halfe an houre after seven a clock at night, we seeing the enemy would not charge us, we resolved by the help of God, to charge them, and so the signe being given, we marched down to the charge…

As was customary, both sides had an identifying token and 'field word'. The Allied troops wore[4] 'a white Paper or handkerchiffe in our hats: our word was 'God with us.' The Enemies signal was to be without bands and skarfes. Their word was 'God and the King.'

The Allied first line was probably only about 600 yards away from the Royalist skirmish line, and could hope to reach it without suffering more than two or three musketry discharges, and perhaps one shot from each of the enemy light guns, assuming them to have been loaded. Speed was of the essence, and as we shall see, some of the foot possibly broke ranks in order to cover the ground as quickly as possible.

According to Ashe:[5]

> Our Army in its severall parts moving downe the Hill, was like unto so many thicke clouds, having divided themselves into Brigades, consisting of eight hundred, one thousand, twelve hundred, fifteen hundred men in a Brigade. And our Brigades of Horse, consisting some of three, and some of foure Troopes.

First to make contact, however, were probably Cromwell's forces on the left.[6] 'We came down the Hill in the bravest order, and with the greatest resolution, that was ever seen…'

It should not be thought that Cromwell's cavalry were engaging in the kind of hell-for-leather charge beloved of Hollywood film-makers. A well-conducted attack by disciplined cavalry such as Cromwell's troopers was a much more deliberate, almost ponderous affair. A Parliamentarian cavalry officer, Capt. John Vernon, writing in 1644, describes the formation which will have been employed:[7]

> All the Troops are to be drawn up into battalia, each [division] being not above three deepe, likewise each troop must be at least a hundred paces distance behind each other for the better avoiding of disorder, those troops that are to give the first charge being drawn up into battail as before, are to be at their closer order, every left-hand man's right knee must be closed locked under his right-hand man's left ham. In this order they are to advance toward the Enemy with an easy pace, firing their Carbines at a convenient distance, always aiming at their enemie's brest or lower, because the powder is of an elevating nature, then drawing near the Enemy they are with their right hands to take forth one of their pistols out of their houlsters, and holding the lock uppermost firing as before, always reserving one Pistol ready charged, spann'd and primed in your houlsters in case of a retreat. I have shewn before, having thus fired the troops are to charge the Enemy in full Career, but in good order, with their swords fastened with a Riband or the like unto their wrists, for fear of losing out of their hand, if they should chance to miss their blow, placing the pommel on their thigh, keeping still in close order, locked as before.

At about the same time that Cromwell closed with Byron's first line, dragoons, possibly John Lilburne's Eastern Association Regiment, attacked musketeers in the cross-ditch on Byron's left, whilst some light guns which had been brought forward opened fire on two Royalist pieces which had been positioned on some slightly rising ground, known as Rye Hill, behind Byron's position. The dragoons:[8] 'acted their part so well that at this first assault they beat the enemy from the ditch, and shortly after killed a great many.'

The young Horſe-man,
O R,
The honeſt plain-dealing CAVALIER.

Wherein is plainly demonſtrated , by figures and other-
wiſe, the Exerciſe and Diſcipline of the horſe,very uſefull
for all thoſe that deſire the knowledge of
warlike Horſe-man-ſhip.

By JOHN VERNON.

PSAL. 20. 7.

*Some truſt in Chariots, and ſome in Horſes , but we will remember the name of
the Lord our God.*

PRO. 21. 31.

The horſe is prepared againſt the day of battail, but ſafety is of the Lord.

London, Printed by *Andrew Coe* , 1644.

50. Title page of John Vernon's manual for cavalry, published in 1644.
Vernon was a Parliamentarian cavalry officer. The illustration shows two fully armoured
cuirassiers, though by 1644 only some senior officers were probably so equipped.

It may be that the Royalist musketeers had been caught unprepared, but many later writers, including by implication Prince Rupert, would place the blame for what happened next squarely upon Lord Byron.

The future King James II wrote many years later in his *Memoirs*, presumably based on information obtained from Rupert:[9]

> The Prince had positioned him [Byron] very advantageously behind a warren and a slough, with a positive command not to quit his ground, but in that posture only to expect and receive the charge of the enemy... The enemy... must necessarily be much disordered in passing over to him as being to receive the fire of 700 musketeers in their advance to him, which undoubtedly had been very dangerous, if not ruinous, to them.

Rupert's so-called *Diary*, again compiled some time after the events which it described, was equally damning:[10] 'Lord Byron then made a Charge upon Cromwell's horse. Represent here the Posture the P. put the forces in and how by the improper charge of the Lord Byron much harm was done.'

Other accounts imputed some sort of treachery or incompetence to Urry, in command of Byron's first line.

Despite this apparent weight of evidence, the case against Byron is not in fact watertight. Whatever Rupert may later have claimed, the ditch at the point where it ran in front of Byron's line was not a serious obstacle. There may have been little more than some water-logged ground before the Royalist position. Accounts of Cromwell's attack make no mention of the ditch presenting a serious obstacle to his advance, nor that the Parliamentarians were engaged with the Royalists until they had actually crossed over whatever barrier existed. It is perhaps more likely that Urry and the first line, hastily mounted, and perhaps still in some disorder, engaged the enemy just after they had crossed the ditch or boggy ground. A number of their musketeers had already been dispersed by the Allied dragoons. What happened next may well have been more a consequence of Byron's first line being overwhelmed by weight of numbers in the 'shoving match' which followed rather than as the result of any failings of Byron and Urry. For the 800 men of Byron's leading divisions faced some 1,500 opponents in Cromwell's first line.

This initial encounter may have lasted only about 10–15 minutes and receives brief coverage in contemporary accounts. According to Lionel Watson, who was probably involved:[11]

> Our front divisions of Horse charged their front, Lieutenant Generall Cromwell's division of three hindred Horse, in which himselfe was in Person, charged the first division of Prince Rupert's in which himselfe was in person. The rest of ours charged other divisions of theirs, but with such admirable valour, as it was to the astonishment of all the old Souldiers of the Army.

But although Byron's first line, with Urry's small regiment reportedly the first to break, was thrown back in disorder, and part of it perhaps routed, the battle on this wing was still to be decided.

To Cromwell's right, the two brigades of Eastern Association foot under the command of Maj.-Gen. Lawrence Crawford also initially made good progress. Watson wrote of their advance:[12] 'In a moment we were passed the ditch into the Moore, upon equall grounds with the enemy, our men going in a running march.'

In order to preserve their formation, infantry normally advanced at a rate of about seventy paces a minute, but Crawford evidently pushed his men rather faster. He hoped thus to minimise their time under fire, and give the Royalists as little chance as possible to recover from their initial surprise. He was also aided by the ditch separating the cultivated ground from the moor being virtually non-existent at this point.[13]

52. Contemporary print of infantry deployed for battle. Note the officers issuing commands and the drummers to transmit orders. Unusually in the Civil War, except in the Scots forces, a body of mounted lancers are stationed in support.

Opposite 51. Cavalry action as depicted in John Vernon's *The Young Horseman* (1644). On the right, a body of cavalry, under attack from front and flank, is routing. Note that the front ranks of opposing troops are firing their pistols.

Upon the advancing of the Earl of Manchester's Foote, after short firings on both sides, we caused the enemy to quit their hedge in a disorderly manner, where they left behind them four Drakes.

Based on the evidence of De Gomme's plan, the Eastern Association foot will have come up against the Royalist infantry tertia formed by Rupert and Byron's regiments, about 1,500 strong. The Royalists would have been outnumbered by about two to one, and may already have been in difficulties as a result of having their right flank threatened by Cromwell's horse as it pushed back the first line of Byron's cavalry. In consequence the Royalist foot tertia, possibly also under attack from the Allied dragoons who had cleared the cross-ditch, may have begun to pivot in a northwesterly direction, which would in turn have made its left flank vulnerable to Crawford's attack.

The outcome seems to have been that the Rupert/Byron tertia broke quickly, allowing Crawford to begin to threaten the right flank of the next formation in the front line of the Royalist infantry, the brigade of troops from Ireland under Henry Warren.

By now the remaining Allied foot were also in action:[14]

The lord Fairfax his Briggade on our right hand did also beat off the Enemy from the hedges before them, driving them from their Cannon, being two drakes and one Demi-Culvering.

This success was far from decisive. It seems unlikely that the Allied foot paused during their advance in order to fire, relying on the weight of their superior numbers to drive the line of Royalist skirmishers from the hedgerow. It is also unlikely that the latter put up any very serious resistance, firing possibly only one or two volleys before abandoning their cannon and falling back on the Royalist front line, perhaps 200 yards north of the hedge.

The Scots foot on the Allied right centre also initially gained some ground. They were opposed by two divisions of foot from Ireland formed from the weak regiments of Richard Gibson and Sir Michael Earnley, and the relatively strong regiment of Henry Tillier. The Scots, possibly with a slight superiority in numbers, as some of their second line units came up in support, appear to have had an advantage in the opening encounter.[15]

Orders being given to advance, the Battell was led on by General Hamilton [Alexander Hamilton, Leven's artillery commander] Liutenant-Generall Baylie, and Major-General Crauford: the Reserve being committed to the trust of Generall Major Lumsdaine: there was a great Ditch between the Enemy and us, which ran along the front of the Battel, only between the Earle of Manchester's Foot and the enemy there was a plain; in the Ditch the enemy had placed foure Brigades of their best Foot; which upon the advance of our Battell were forced to give ground, being gallantly assaulted by the Earl of

53. A musketeer. This character carries his ammunition in a powder bag and wears
a woollen 'Monmouth' cap, which were reasonably weather-proof and cheap to produce.

Lindsie's regiment, the Lord Maitland's, Cassilis, and Kelhead's. Generall
Major Crauford having overwinged the enemy set upon their flank, and did
very good execution upon the enemy, which gave occasion to the Scottish
Foote to advance and pass the Ditch.

The infantry battle now entered a more serious phase. The Allied infantry commanders must have hoped to get their men across the ditch quickly enough, and in suffi-
ciently good order, to hit the Royalist front line before its commanders could get
their men into good enough order to meet them. In that way a snowballing rout
might commence.

Such an outcome depended on the vigour and determination with which the
Allied foot pressed on, the danger being that poorly motivated troops might slow
down or halt, and the sort of ineffective exchange of fire take place which James II
witnessed at Edgehill in 1642:[16] '…each [the opposing foot] as if by mutual consent
retired some few paces, and they stuck down their coulours, continuing to fire at one
another even till night…'

Such encounters, whilst prolonged, tended to inflict few casualties, and the
advantage would lie with whichever side was first able to bring up reserves and

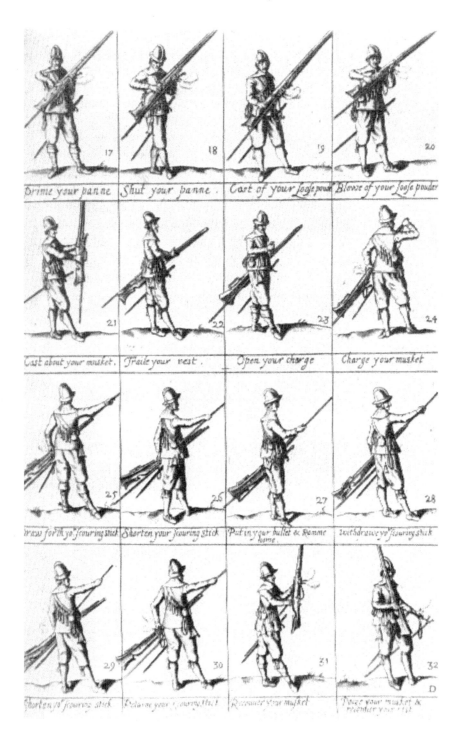

54. Musket drill. Although procedures such as these laid down for the loading and firing of muskets were elaborate and lengthy, in battle situations they were usually considerably simplified.

launch a renewed assault. On the Allied side the Scots foot in particular seem to have been quite slow in moving up, whilst not only were many of Rupert's 'Irish' infantry in his first line more experienced than their opponents, but some at least of the seasoned northern foot in their second line were now advancing in support. Deployed as they were in chequer-board style formation, the northerners were able to move into the intervals between the divisions of the Royalist first line to join in the battle and launch a counterattack.

By now as the intensity of the fighting mounted, confusion was spreading along the 2-mile battlefront; a captain known to us only as 'W.H.', but probably an officer in the Army of the Eastern Association, remembered:[17]

> ...then the main bodyes joining, made such a noise with shot and clamour of shouting that we lost our eares, and the smoke of powder was so thick that we saw no light but what proceeded from the mouth of guns.

And, as the Allied infantry in the centre began to stall, their horse on the right were running into serious trouble.

Even before they came into contact with Goring's horse, Sir Thomas Fairfax and his men were facing difficulties with the terrain. The area immediately to the west of the village of Long Marston, across which they had to advance, was partially enclosed with hedgrows, and further west, towards Moor Lane, the approach was evidently made difficult by gorse and possibly boggy ground. For the horse on the

55. Sir Edward Widdrington commanded a reserve brigade of Newcastle's Northern Horse at Marston Moor.

56. Army encampment. This probably gives a good impression of a typical Civil War encampment. Note the trader's hut (right) and the improvised tents of the soldiers. Many soldiers' wives and women camp followers accompanied armies despite official disapproval. The Allied siege lines at York may have resembled this scene.

right of Fairfax's front line, the most feasible way of approaching the enemy position on the moor was to advance in column down what is now Atterwith Lane, and then to deploy on the open ground of the moor immediately beyond the ditch. Those troops entering the moor by means of the lane would at least have the advantage of the breach it made in the ditch at that point. Elsewhere Fairfax's men faced a much more formidable barrier, with perhaps a 6ft-high bank forming the demarcation line between cultivated land and moor with a steep drop on its northern side.

It would have been a difficult and dangerous manoeuvre in any case, and, against an opponent of the calibre of Goring, it was a recipe for disaster. The Northern Horse, thanks to their attached troops of dragoons, which were added to the parties of 'commanded' musketeers which Rupert had deployed, were particularly strong in firepower, and according to one account, Goring had lined a hedge on one side of Atterwith Lane and a ditch on the other with musketeers.

Fairfax apparently placed some newly levied troops at the head of his advance, which may have been with a view to their diverting some of the enemy fire from his more seasoned men. But they were also likely to break more quickly.

If Goring's men had in fact stood down, they seem to have had time to resume their positions before the Parliamentarians reached them, and opened up a hail of musketry whose intensity is reflected in the literally hundreds of musket balls found in recent times embedded in the northern side of the bank.[18]

A Parliamentarian account describes the outcome:[19]

The Right wing of our Foot [sic] had severall misfortunes, for betwixt them and the enemy there was no passage but at a narrow Lane, where they could not march above 3 or 4 in front, upon the one side of the Lane was a Ditch, and on the other aine Hedge, both whereof were lined with Musquetiers. Notwithstanding Sir Thomas Fairfax charged gallantly, but the enemy keeping themselves in a body, and receiving them by threes and foures as they marched out of the Lane, and (by what mistake I know not) Sir Thomas Fairfax his new

57. Cornet of Col. John Lambert. This colour may have been carried at Marston Moor.

111

leavied regiment, being in the Van, they wheeled about, and being hotly pursued by the enemy, came back upon the Lord Fairfax Foot....

Sir Thomas Fairfax's own account of the disaster is interesting, if understandably evasive in places:[20]

...our Right Wing had not, all, so good success, by reason of the whins, and ditches which we were to pass over before we could get to the Enemy, which put us into great disorder. Notwithstanding, I drew up a body of 400 Horse. But because the intervals of [Royalist] Horse, in this Wing only, were lined with Musquetiers; which did us much hurt with their shot: I was necessitated to charge them [before the remainder of his horse could deploy in support]. We were a long time engaged one with another, but at last we routed that part of their Wing. We charged and pursued them a good waye towards Yorke.

Myselfe only returned presently to get to the men I left behind me. But that part of the Enemy which stood, perceiving the disorder they were in, had charged and routed them, before I could get to them. So that the good success we had at first was eclipsed much by this bad conclusion.

58. Lt-Col. Henry Constable served with Newcastle's Northern Horse under Sir Edward Widdrington. His device, which might have been expected also to have included a cross, was popular among Roman Catholics such as Constable.

Filling out the details of these accounts, what seems to have happened is roughly as follows. Sir Thomas Fairfax managed to deploy the bulk of his own regiment, who were not the new-levied troops described in the Parliamentarian *True Account*, onto the moor at the point where Atterwith Lane entered it. They charged and routed a division of Royalist horse, possibly the 200 men under Col. Francis Carnaby, and the bulk of Fairfax's division headed off in pursuit.

Sir Thomas's own troops did not escape unscathed:[21] 'The captain of my own Troop was shot in the arm. My Cornet had both his hands cut, that rendered him ever more unserviceable.'

But meanwhile the remainder of his first two lines of horse, about 2,500 men, had met with total disaster. Col. John Lambert, commanding the second line, saw that to attempt an advance along Atterwith Lane in support of Sir Thomas would merely compound the initial confusion, 'so charged in another place' – probably in the area between the Atterwith and Moor Lanes. His men came under the same intense fire which had hit Fairfax's first line, and Lambert's major, a relative of Sir Thomas, suffered thirty wounds. The Parliamentarians, including Sir Thomas's brother Charles Fairfax's newly raised regiment, and some poor-quality Lancashire horse, were already reeling under the effect of the Royalist musket fire when Goring, with the remainder of his first and possibly part of his second line, charged the enemy as they struggled to deploy on to the moor.

The rout was rapid and total. Parliamentarian losses, particularly among officers, were heavy. Charles Fairfax, 'being deserted of his men', was mortally wounded, and another regimental commander, Col. Sir Hugh Bethell, also seriously injured, as were many junior officers.

Goring, probably with Langdale's brigade and the Newark horse, drove on to attack Fairfax's third line, the 1,000 Scottish horse who had evidently not advanced far enough to become entangled in the initial debacle. The Scots seem to have put up stronger, though probably brief, resistance:[22]

> ...the two squadrons of Balgonie's regiment being divided by the enemy each from the other, one of them being Lanciers, charged a regiment of the enemye's foot, and put them wholly to the rout, and after joyn'd with the left wing: the Earle of Eglington's regiment maintained their ground (most of the enemy going on in pursuit of the Horse and Foote that fled) but with the losse of four Lieutenants the Lieutenant-Colonell, Major, and Eglington's Sonne being deadly wounded.

The entire first stage of the action on the Allied right can only have occupied a short space of time, perhaps no more than 20 minutes, if we are to judge by the implied timescale of the only surviving account by a Royalist participant, Col. Sir Philip Monckton, who was in Goring's first line. As the Parliamentarians began their advance, Monckton, who had a reputation for rash displays of bravery, decided to put on a performance to encourage his men:[23]

59. Sir Thomas Fairfax,
showing the scar from the wound he suffered at Marston Moor.

60. John Lambert (1619–83). He served with Lord Fairfax's Northern forces from 1642
and distinguished himself at the Siege of Hull (1643) and at Nantwich (1644).
He served as Sir Thomas Fairfax's second-in-command at Marston Moor. Later one
of Cromwell's major-generals, Lambert played a major role at the battles of Preston,
Dunbar, Inverkeithing and Worcester.

I had my horse shot under me as I caracoled at the head of the body I
commanded, and so near the enemy that I could not be mounted again, but
charged on foot, and beat Sir Hugh Bethell's regiment of horse, who was
wounded and dismounted, and my servant brought me his horse. When I was
mounted upon him the wind driving the smoke so as I could not see what was
become of the body I commanded, which went in pursuit of the enemy…

Though some of the Scots horse remained on the field, they were too few to prevent
the second line of Goring's horse, under Sir Charles Lucas, turning their attention to
the Allied foot.

As the Allied attack began, the sound of firing had alerted the Royalist
commanders settling down in the rear to supper. We shall consider Prince
Rupert's reaction later, but the Marquis of Newcastle had just settled in his coach
when the fighting commenced.[24]

Not long had my Lord been there, but he heard a great noise and thunder of shooting, which gave him notice of the armies being engaged. Whereupon he immediately put on his arms, and was no sooner got on horseback, but he beheld a dismal sight of the horse of his Majesty's right wing which out of a panic fear had left the field, and run away with all the speed they could; and though my Lord made them stand once, yet they immediately betook themselves to their heels again, and killed even those of their own party that endeavoured to stop them. The left wing in the meantime, commanded by those two valiant persons, the Lord Goring and Sir Charles Lucas, having the better of the enemys' right wing, which they beat back most valiantly three times, and made their general retreat, insomuch that they sounded victory.

In this confusion my Lord (accompanied only with his brother Sir Charles Cavendish, Major Scott, Captain Mazine, and his page) hastening to see in what posture his own regiment was, met with a troop of gentlemen volunteers, who formerly had chosen him their captain... to whom my Lord spake after this manner. 'Gentlemen' said he: 'you have done me the honour to choose me your captain, and now is the fittest time that I may do you service; wherefore if you will follow me, I shall lead you on the best I can, and show you the way to your own honour... [They] went on with the greatest courage, and passing through two bodies of foot, engaged with each other not at forty yards' distance, received not the least hurt, although they fired quick upon each other, but marched towards a Scots regiment of foot, which they charged and routed: in which encounter my Lord himself killed three with his own page's half-lead sword, for he had no other left him; and though all the gentlemen in particular offered him their swords, yet my Lord refused to take a sword of any of them. At last, after they had passed through this regiment of foot, a pikeman made a stand to the whole troop; and though my Lord charged him twice or thrice, yet he could not enter him; but the troops despatched him soon.

In these encounters my Lord had not the least hurt, though several were slain about him...

Newcastle no doubt performed the role of a gallant soldier worthily enough, but he might have been better employed in trying to get some sort of grip on the overall Royalist command situation. He may have felt that his subordinates were well-enough qualified to act for themselves, and indeed several of them were in the process of demonstrating exactly that.

The initial onslaught by Lord Fairfax's and the Scottish foot had now been halted, and the Royalist infantry, reinforced by some of the northern units in their second line, launched a spirited counterattack which quickly gained ground. Lord Fairfax's foot,[25] 'being received by Marquesse Newcastle's regiment of foot, and being by them furiously assaulted, did make a retreat in some disorder...'

Sir William Blakiston, with his 800-strong brigade of Northern cavalry, had been placed in support of the first line of Royalist foot. Blakiston, a Durham man,

61. Sir Charles Lucas (d.1648). A professional soldier who, according to Clarendon, was 'bred in the Low Countries, and always amongst the horse, so that he had little conversation in that Court, where great civility was practised and learnt.' He served in the Second Scots War and fought at Powick Bridge and Edeghill, and with the Oxford Army during 1643. Lucas was exchanged in the winter of 1644, and served as Governor of Berkeley Castle. He joined the Royalist cause again in 1648 and was shot in the surrender of Colchester for breaking the terms of his parole at the end of the First Civil War.

displayed considerable courage on several occasions during the war, and was also a highly capable cavalry commander. He was quick to seize his opportunity on this occasion. Seeing Fairfax's men reeling, Blakiston charged them through an interval in the foot with his brigade of horse, and routed them, and (perhaps joined by Newcastle and his troop), broke the Scots foot to their rear, driving on at least as far as the lower crest of the ridge. Behind him the triumphant Royalist foot surged forward to the ditch, re-taking their lost guns. Lord Fairfax was himself evidently with his broken troops, and joined in the rout, not drawing rein until he reached his home at Cawood, where, not being expected, he retired to bed without any supper!

At the same time that Blakiston launched his attack, Sir Charles Lucas with the second – and perhaps part of the first – lines of Goring's horse, was preparing a larger onslaught on the Scots foot to Fairfax's right. Some Scots units had already been disordered by Sir Thomas Fairfax's fleeing horse, and now they were under attack from Lucas's men on their right flank and the Royalist foot to their front.

The rout seems to have infected Hamilton's Scots brigade to Lord Fairfax's right. These were probably already getting the worst of their encounter with Tillier's Greencoats, and the two regiments, Hamilton's and Rae's, which formed the brigade now broke and ran. The panic spread to the Scots second line, which should have moved forward to fill the gap, and they joined in the flight.[26]

> ...those that ran away shew themselves most baslie. I [Lumsden] commanding the battell was on the head of your Lordship's regiment [Loudon's] and Buccleuch's, but they carried not themselves as I would have wised, neither could I prevail with them. For these that fled never came to chairge with the enemis, but were so possessed with ane pannick feare that they ran for example to others and no enemie following, which gave the enemie occasion to chairge them...

The Earl of Leven himself made desperate but unavailing attempts to stem the rout. He yelled desperately to the fleeing infantry:[27] 'Although you run from your Enemies, yet leave not your Generall, though you flie from them, yet forsake not mee'

Finding his pleas ignored Leven, though, according to a later face-saving version, only on the entreaties of his staff that he save himself, joined in the flight, riding without pause through the night until he reached the safety of Leeds.

As the Scots right began to crumble, Lucas threw in a series of probably ill-co-ordinated assaults intended to complete the process.[28]

> Sir Charles Lucas and Generall-Major Porter having thus divided all our Horse on that wing, assaulted the Scottish Foot upon their Flanks, so that they had the Foot upon their front, and the whole Cavalry of the enemie's left wing to fight with, whom they encountered with so much courage and resolution, that they enterlined their Musquetiers with Pikemen; they made the Enemies' Horse, notwithstanding for all the assistance they had of their foot, at two severall assaults to give ground; and in this hot dispute with both they continued almost an houre, still maintaininge theire grounde; Lieutenant-Generall Baily, and Generall Major Lumsden (who both gave good evidence of their courage and skill) perceiving the great weight of the battell to lye sore upon the Earl of Linsies, and Lord Maitlands regiment, send up a reserve, for their assistance, after which the Enemies Horse having made a third assault upon them, had almost put them in some disorder; but the Earl of Lindsey and Lieutenant-Colonell Pitscottie, Lieutenant-Colonel to the Lord Maitland's Regiment, behaved themselves so gallantly, that they quickly made the Enemies Horse to retreat, killed Sir Charles Lucas his Horse, tooke him Prisoner, and gained ground upon the Foote.

The action had been extremely hotly contested, and the stand by the Lindsey/Maitland brigade bought the Allies vital time. But, despite the evident intensity of the fighting, the available Royalist horse, perhaps 1,000–1,500 men,

62. A Scots 'frame gun'. So called after their mounts, these light pieces, firing shot of 3lb or less, were employed mainly in an anti-personnel role. Easily dismantled, they could be transported on packhorses. Although large numbers of frame guns were present at Marston Moor, contemporary accounts make no mention of their use there.

proved too few to break the enemy. Once the gallant Scots were reinforced by reserves, probably brought across by Lumsden from the Scottish foot stationed in the second and third lines on the left centre, the immediate crisis here was over.

But at about 8.30 p.m., an hour after fighting had begun, an impartial onlooker might well have laid odds on a Royalist victory. Apart from a handful of Scots, and some of Fairfax's men chasing fugitives towards York, the entire Allied right wing of horse was in flight, with Goring and part of his horse pursuing them towards the Allied baggage train. Nearly half the Allied foot, including at least half of Lord Fairfax's infantry and a similar proportion of the Scots were routed. The Royalist infantry had regained their lost ground, and were now holding their own.

It was only on the left that the Allies seemed still to have grounds for hope. Cromwell had successfully disposed of Byron's first line, and Crawford's foot were making some progress. However Rupert had launched a counterattack, and fighting was fierce. It was here, in the next half hour, that the battle of Marston Moor would be decided.

7

MARSTON MOOR: PHASE 2, 8.30 P.M.–MIDNIGHT

After over an hour of fighting, dense clouds of choking smoke created by black-powder combat, slow to disperse on what was probably a still evening, had brought a premature onset of near-darkness over Marston Moor. Through the smoke, usually in ignorance of events beyond their immediate vicinity, bodies of horse and foot continued to grapple. The sound of musketry and occasional cannon fire, and the rattle of steel engulfed shouted orders, identifying field words, and the cries of the wounded.

Hundreds, perhaps thousands, of men, mainly though by no means all Allied troops, were in flight from the battlefield. Some of the fugitives, heading south, brought with them confused stories of disaster which gave birth to reports and rumours of a great Royalist victory.

Arriving on the scene in the midst of this chaos was Arthur Trevor, Rupert's agent, bound from Lancashire with a message for the prince from Ormonde.[1]

> I could not meet the Prince until the battle was joined, and in the fire, smoke and confusion of that day, I knew not for my soul whither to incline. The runaways on both sides were so many, so breathless, so speechless, and so full of fears that I should not have taken them for men, but by their motion which still served them very well; not a man being able to give me the least hope where the Prince was to be found both armies being mingled, both horse and foot; no side keeping their own posts.
>
> In this horrible distraction did I coast the country; here meeting with a shoal of Scots crying 'Wey's us, we are all undone'; and so full of lamentation and mourning, as if their day of doom had overtaken them, and from which they knew not whither to fly: and anon I met with a ragged troope of horse reduced to four and a Cornet; by and by with a little foot officer without a hat, band, sword, or indeed anything but feet and so much tongue as would serve to enquire the way to the next garrisons, which (to say the truth) were

63. Contemporary illustration of a cavalry engagement,
conveying something of the chaotic nature of such encounters.

well filled with the stragglers on both sides within a few hours, though they
lay distant from the place of the fight 20 or 30 miles.

Some of the fiercest fighting was now taking place on the Allied left, between
Cromwell's and Byron's horse, and to understand this we need to go back to the
actions of Prince Rupert at the beginning of the battle.

Choosing not to dine with Newcastle, a decision which perhaps better than any
illustrates the fraught relationship between the two senior Royalist commanders,
Rupert retired to eat supper with the men of his lifeguard, stationed with the
Royalist reserve.[2]

...so that when the alarum was given, he was set upon the earth at meat a
pretty distance from his troops, and many of the horsemen were dismounted
and laid on the ground with their horses [bridles] in their hands.

Upon the alarum the Prince mounted to horse and [went] galloping up to
the right wing...

In fact it is unlikely that this happened as quickly as Cholmley suggests. Rupert, who could have seen little detail of the initial fighting from his position near White Syke Close, must certainly have paused long enough to glean some initial impression of how the fight was going, possibly by sending out riders to each part of the field. He will have learnt that Goring was more than holding his own, and that the situation in the centre was generally stable. Probably within 15 minutes it would have become obvious that the immediate crisis was on the right, and Rupert took command of his reserve, consisting of his lifeguard and Lord Widdrington's brigade, and headed in that direction. He has been criticised for thus abandoning the possibility of exercising overall direction of the battle, but in fact, once the small reserve was committed, there was very little left that he could have done. The only other troops not involved were those northern foot still

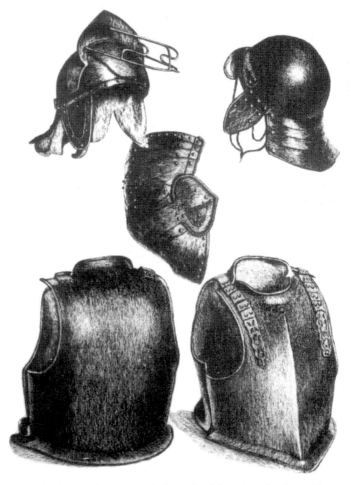

64. Armour of a 'harquebusier', including shoulder piece, back and breast plates and 'pot' or 'lobster-tail' helmet with moveable face guard. Armour of this sort was cheaper than the best-quality buff coats.

coming up, and Eythin was better known to them and more likely than Rupert to obtain their co-operation.

By the time that the prince neared the fighting on his right, Byron's first line had evidently already collapsed, and the rot had spread to Rupert's own 500-strong regiment on the left of the second line. Rupert:[3]

> ...met his own regiment turning their backs to the enemy which was a thing so strange and unusual he said 'swounds, do you run, follow me', so facing about, he led them to a charge.

Cromwell's men were now discovering that, despite their easy initial success, victory was by no means assured. Byron had some 1,400 men in his second line, versus perhaps 2,600 men still available in the first two Parliamentarian lines. Cromwell's first line at least will have been disordered by the initial encounter, and at this point the Royalists counterattacked.

Lionel Watson admitted:[4]

> Cromwell's own division had a hard pull of it; for they were charged by Rupert's bravest men, both in Front and Flank, they stood at sword's point a pretty while, hacking at one another...

Cromwell's men must have had to contend with Rupert's regiment, possibly reinforced by the prince and his lifeguard, to their front, and evidently with a flank attack by Marcus Trevor and his 400 troopers. At some stage in this encounter Cromwell was slightly wounded by a pistol shot graze to his neck, in one version an accidental injury inflicted by one of his own men, which seems quite possible, or in a tradition of the Trevor family, by a shot fired by Marcus Trevor.

Exactly what happened next is a matter of continuing dispute. It seems likely that Cromwell retired briefly from the field in order to have his wound dressed, possibly at a nearby cottage in Tockwith. In his absence, Comm.-Gen. Bartholomew Vermuyden might have been expected to have assumed command, but sources are silent on this point. The episode became the focus of fierce controversy, centred around accusations levelled against Cromwell by his Presbyterian opponents, notably Lawrence Crawford and Denzil Holles. The burden of the complaints was that Cromwell lost his nerve, and that Crawford and Leslie had to take over command and save the situation.

Denzil Holles, the most outspoken of the critics, wrote:

> Lieutenant-General Cromwell had the impudence to assume much of the honour to himself... my friend Cromwell had neither part nor lot in the business. For I have several times heard it from Crawford's own mouth that when the whole army at Marston Moor was in a fair possibility to be

65. Nineteenth-century artist's impression of the Battle of Marston Moor.

routed, and a great part of it running, he saw the body of horse of that Brigade standing still, and, so to his seeming, doubtful which way to charge; backward or forward, when he came up to them in a great passion, reviling them in the name of poltroons and cowards, and asked them if they would stand still and see the day lost? Whereupon Cromwell shewed himself, and in a pitiful voice said: 'Major-General, what shall I do?' Crawford, begging his superior officer's pardon, told Cromwell: 'Sir, if you charge, not all is lost.'

Cromwell responded that he was wounded, and of this Holles reports:[5] 'his great wound being but a little burn in the neck by the accidental going off behind him of one of his soldiers' pistols.'

According to Holles, Crawford sent Cromwell off the field and took over command himself.

Other accounts offer slightly different versions, though along similar lines. One has Cromwell wounded in the neck during he first charge:[6] 'though it was not very dangerous (being but a rake in the neck), yet the pistol being discharged soe neare, that the powder burnt his face and troubled his eyes.' In this version Cromwell stayed on the field though he withdrew from the front line.

In another critical account:[7] 'Cromwell did not at all appear in the heat of the business, but having at first a little skar, kept off till the worst was past.'

However, Lord Saye, a supporter of Cromwell, asserted that:[8] '...it is known that [Cromwell] charged in the head of those Regiments of Horse in my Lord Manchester's army, which Horse he commanded...'

Douglas, a Scot writing immediately after the battle, said that Cromwell:[9] '...charged verie well, [but] at the first was lightly hurt, went off, and came out againe.'

It may be possible to reconcile these differing accounts into an approximation of the truth. Cromwell, though undoubtedly a great trainer of men and eventually a self-taught strategist of near-genius, was in 1644 a man in late middle age, with no pre-war military training or experience. There is nothing to suggest that he either relished, or was particularly adept in, hand-to-hand combat, for which both age and lack of training would have left him at a disadvantage. At Winceby in the previous October, he had been unhorsed early in the fight, and is not mentioned in an active role thereafter. He seems to have been willing, if not relishing the task, to expose himself to danger in moments of crisis, such as the episode during the storming of Drogheda in 1649, when he rallied wavering Parliamentarian foot. But it is quite possible to envisage his being badly shaken by the wound he suffered at Marston Moor, and temporarily rendered unfit to make speedy decisions, perhaps even briefly leaving the field to recover. What is difficult to accept is that his horse would have been left paralysed by his temporary absence. The Eastern Association cavalry had a number of experienced regimental commanders capable of taking over in such a situation.

Lawrence Crawford's second-hand account (he was dead by the time Holles aired his accusations) is difficult to credit. Crawford would surely have been fully occupied in leading his foot in the tough fighting in which they were involved, and even if he had ridden over to confer with Cromwell, would hardly have been in a position to command the horse as well as his own men.

The most probable explanation of what happened is that Cromwell, shaken by his injury, did briefly retire to have it dressed. At the same time he very wisely consulted with one of the most experienced officers with him, David Leslie, the Scots lieutenant-general of horse, whose 1,000 horse, forming Cromwell's third line, were not yet engaged. Between them they came up with the far from revolutionary tactic of Leslie making a flank attack on the Royalists whilst Cromwell's men continued to engage them frontally.

Contemporary writers pay tribute to the stubborn resistance of Byron's second line, which had been reinforced by Rupert and Trevor's regiments, the prince himself with his lifeguard and possibly Lord Widdrington's brigade. This would have given them a total of in the region of 2,000 men, opposed by up to 3,000 Eastern Association troopers. The Royalists included some veteran soldiers, especially Rupert's units and the regiments of Lord Molyneux and Sir Thomas Tyldesley, some of whom had served with the Oxford Army at Edgehill and the First Battle of Newbury.

The Parliamentarian writer Thomas Stockdale admitted that Rupert and Trevor's counterattack had some success:[10] 'Yet after a little time the Earl of

66. Contemporary Parliamentarian cartoon showing Rupert hiding in the bean field.
Nearby is the body of his dog, 'Boye', and his captured sumpter horses,
supposedly carrying various Roman Catholic religious items.

Manchester's horse were repulsed by fresh supplies of the enemies, and forced to retreat in some disorder.'

The Royalists lacked the advantage in numbers to exploit their success, and a not necessarily particularly bloody stalemate followed as the two densely packed masses of horsemen hacked at each other, trying to force a gap in their opponents' ranks.

According to the Parliamentarian Lord Saye:[11]

> ...the enemy's horse, being many of them, if not the greatest part, gentlemen, stood very firm a long while, coming to a close fight with the sword, and standing like an iron wall, so that they were not easily broken; if the Scots light but weak nags had undertaken that work, they had never been able to stand a charge or endure the shock of the enemy's horse, both horse and men being very good, and fighting desperately enough.

It is uncertain how long the deadlock lasted; from first to last the fight on the Allied right continued for about 40 minutes. But, as the outnumbered Royalist horse began to tire, Leslie struck the decisive blow, wheeling his 1,000 Scots horse in against the Cavaliers' right flank. It was too much for Rupert's exhausted troopers,

67. Sir Henry Slingsby (1602–58). Of Yorkshire gentry stock, Slingsby had served in the Low Countries, 'A commendable way of breeding for a young Gentleman.' He raised a regiment of foot in 1642 and took part in the Siege of Hull. He served later with the Northern Horse and in 1658 was beheaded for treason for his part in the Royalist rising of 1655.

who quickly broke. Leslie[12] 'charged the enemie's horse (with whom L.Generall Cromwell was engaged) upon the flank, and in a very short space the enemie's whole cavalry was routed.'

As the Royalists reeled under Leslie's attack, Cromwell's horse to their front took advantage of the disorder, and[13] 'brake through them, scattering them before him like a little dust.'

As his men routed, Rupert:[14] 'being separated from his troope, and surrounded by the enemy, killed 4 or 5 with his owne hands, and at last hee brake strangely through them…'

According to Parliamentary propaganda, Rupert was forced to hide in a bean field to escape capture. This was a common claim in such situations, and cannot be verified, though there were cultivated patches on the fringes of the moor.

Once the rout began, there was no stopping the fleeing Royalist horse. Sir Henry Slingsby, who was perhaps with Widdrington's men, watched them[15] 'fly along by Wilstrop woodside, as fast and as thick could be.'

Most of the fugitives seem to have headed northeastwards, in the direction of York, and some, as we shall see, would eventually rally, but their active role in the battle was at an end.

Cromwell and Leslie now worked closely together to exploit their success. Leslie seems to have taken up the initial pursuit. According to Lord Saye:[16]

Herein indeed was the good service David Leslie did that day with his little light Scotch nags… that when a regiment of the enemie's was broken he then fell in and followed the chase, doing execution upon them, and keeping them from rallying again and getting into bodies.

Cromwell kept his own troopers 'close together in firm bodies',[17] and took,[18]

...special care to see it observed that the regiments of horse, when they had broken the a regiment of the enemie's, should not divide, and in pursuit of the enemie break their order, but keep themselves still together in bodies to charge the other regiments of the enemy which stood firm.

Some troops, perhaps part of Vermuyden's second line, were detached to pursue the Royalists, mainly to prevent them from re-forming, but, as Ashe pointed out, Cromwell kept the bulk of his men in hand for further action:[19] 'Our fore troops did execution to the walls of York, but our body of horse kept their ground.'

As a result Royalist losses in the pursuit were probably not very heavy, but Cromwell must have been beginning to realise that the day was far from won for the Allies, and indeed might yet be lost.

68. Lord Grandison, a captain in Prince Rupert's regiment of horse, was killed at Marston Moor.

He drew his horse up, probably in the area roughly around the northern end of the present Kendal Lane, and tried to discover the situation. Clouds of smoke and general confusion must have made the task difficult, and whilst they were pondering their next move, Cromwell and Leslie were joined by none other than Sir Thomas Fairfax. Fairfax had adventures of his own to relate:[20]

> ...having charged through the Enemy, and my men going after the pursuit; returning back [alone] to go to my other troops, I was gotten in among the Enemy, which stood up and down the Field in several bodies of Horse. So taking the Signal out of my hat, I passed through, for one of their own Commanders; and so got to my Lord of Manchester's Horse in the other Wing; only with a cut in my cheek which was given me in the first charge, and a shot my horse received.

Fairfax is sometimes credited with a key role in the subsequent actions of Cromwell and Leslie, but there is little evidence to support this. Apart from the disaster suffered by his own cavalry, of which he could tell the other commanders, he knew little more than they did regarding the situation on the rest of the field. Sir Thomas himself never made any claims to have influenced subsequent events, and most probably simply rode with Cromwell as a volunteer.

Meanwhile fighting had continued elsewhere. The charge mounted by Sir William Blakiston, possibly joined by Newcastle, had reached the ridge line, where the Royalists may have mauled a regiment of Manchester's foot,[21] 'most of Manchester's blew coats which fought under the bloody colours are cut off.'

Blakiston's men had shot their bolt. Disorganised and exhausted, they came under fire from other Eastern Association foot, and dispersed back on to the moor, to be heard of no more.

Whilst Cromwell had been locked in combat with Rupert and his horse, Goring had been following up his success on the Royalist left. With most of the first line of his cavalry he had swept on up to the crest of the ridge in pursuit of Fairfax's fleeing troopers, who were joined by a large number of Allied foot. The rout was swelled by panic-stricken civilian spectators from neighbouring towns and villages.[22]

> The enemy being in pursuit and chase of retreating men, followed them to our Carriages, but had slain few of them, for indeed they ran away before the enemy charged them.

The Royalists then fell on the Allied baggage train, and some plundering took place, although criticisms that Goring threw away his chance of victory by losing control of his men and allowing them to waste valuable time in looting seem exaggerated. It was notoriously difficult to keep full control of cavalry in a pursuit situation, and Goring, as we shall see, did have partial success in rallying his men. He was not, however, by any means as successful as Cromwell on the other wing.

69. Civilian spectators at the Battle of Naseby. Crowds of local people often gathered to watch battles. At Marston Moor their panic is said to have intensified the rout of Allied troops.

According to the Parliamentarian Thomas Stockdale, the Royalists:[23]

> ...possess themselves first of our Ordinance, and shortly after our carriages also which they first plundered, though afterwards it is conceived they were plundered by our owne Armys, and some of the enemyes horse pursued our flying horse near two myles from the field, soe that in all appearances the day was lost.

Some of the Allied fugitives did not draw rein until they reached Lincoln, Hull, Halifax and Wakefield.

Royalist writers would later criticise Goring for his failure to keep his men under better control:[24]

> Goring was possessed of many of their Ordnance, and if his men had been kept close together, as did Cromwell, and not dispersed themselves in pursuit, in all probability it had come to a drawn battle at worst... but Goring's men were much scattered and dispersed in pursuit before they could know of the defeat of the Prince's right wing...

131

Controlling the northern cavalry, by no means renowned for their discipline, will have been made more difficult by the presence of many small units, brigaded together in *ad hoc* formations. Eventually Goring was probably able to rally about a thousand of his men, and some of Sir Charles Lucas's disorganised and 'blown' horse also probably joined him, but by then the overall position of the Royalists had taken a serious turn for the worse.

On seeing the Eastern Association horse drawing into a body and threatening their right rear and flank, whoever was now in command of the Royalist foot in the vicinity will have attempted to pull them back in a northeasterly direction in order to present a new front. This enabled Crawford's Eastern Association infantry, possibly supported by a few Scots, to push further across the ditch onto the moor proper, and begin to face northeastwards, their left linking up with Cromwell's right.

Some reconstructions have Cromwell and his horse making a largely unopposed passage behind the rear of the Royalist army until they appeared in the position occupied by Goring's cavalry at the start of the battle, but in fact the Allies faced some fierce resistance from bodies of increasingly desperate Royalist foot.

The Eastern Association horse and foot worked in close co-operation as, with the confusion of the battlefield now partially alleviated by the light of a harvest moon, they steadily advanced eastwards, rolling up the Royalist line.

According to Watson:[25]

70. Cornet of Capt. Valentine Walton, Cromwell's nephew, who served in his regiment of horse and was mortally wounded at Marston Moor.

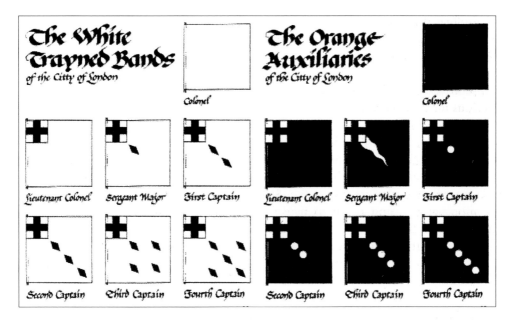

71. A common Civil War flag system in which the rank of the bearer
is indicated by the number of symbols on the individual flag.

Just then, came our Horse and Foot from the chase of their right wing and
seeing the business not well in our right, came in a very good order to a
second charge with all the enemies Horse and Foot that had disordered our
right wing and main battell. And here came the businesse of the day…

The degree of resistance varied. Some of the Lancashire troops, probably Chisenall's
or Tyldesley's foot, threw down their arms and cried for mercy, calling that they were
all pressed men, but others put up a tough fight. Leslie and his horse encountered
some of the troops from Ireland, and[26] 'charged a brigade of Greencoats, whereof
they cut off a great number, and put the rest to rout.'
   The Allies pressed on inexorably:[27]

Our three brigades of foot of the Earle of Manchester's being on our
[Cromwell's cavalry] right hand on we went with great resolution, charging
them so home, one while their Horse then again their Foot.

Judging by the evidence of patterns of located shot and burial pits, some of the
heaviest fighting of the entire battle took place in the area immediately southwest
of Four Lanes Meet. It is possible that the last northern troops to reach the field,
probably up to 1,000 strong and including the Marquis of Newcastle's own
regiment, under Col. Posthumous Kirton, 'a wild and desperate fellow', had not so
far been committed to action. This was an élite unit of the Northern Army, raised
in Northumberland and Durham in 1642. Considerably larger than most of

Newcastle's infantry formations, it had a distinguished record in the action at: Piercebridge in December 1642; Wakefield in May 1643, where, in similar circumstances to those it now faced, it had refused to surrender; and at Adwalton Moor, where the charge of its pikemen had helped win the day for the Royalists. With the Royalist foot being pressed back in increasing confusion towards Hessay and the road to York, Lord Eythin (for it is hard to imagine the northern foot obeying anyone else), probably now ordered Kirton's men to fight a rearguard action to cover the escape of as many troops as possible, and also perhaps give time for Goring's horse to re-form. This, at least, is the most likely explanation for one of the most celebrated actions of the war.

Somewhere in the vicinity of the modern White Syke Close, Cromwell and his horse came up against a massed 'hedgehog' of the northern foot, musketeers firing from beneath the shelter of an array of bristling pikes.

The Scots writer James Somerville said that Cromwell and Leslie had met with no 'great resistance' until they encountered 'the Marquis of Newcastle his battalion of whitecoats', who now opened fire on Cromwell's cavalry, 'first peppering them soundly with their shot.' Cromwell mounted a charge, the Royalists:[28]

> ...stoutly bore up with their pikes, that they could not enter to break them.
> Here the parliament horse received their greatest loss, and a stop for some

72. This Royalist cornet, depicting Parliamentarian leaders as dogs attacking a lion,
was originally carried by the Earl of Carnarvon, killed at the First Battle of Newbury.
As it was captured at Marston Moor, it was evidently taken over by another Royalist officer.

73. Pike drill. On the march, unless combat was expected, pikes were often carried in wagons. Some of the positions shown here were for ceremonial rather than combat use.

time to their hoped-for victory, and that only by the stout resistance of this gallant battalion.

Cromwell could not afford to be delayed without risking an enemy recovery. He detached Frazer's dragoons, probably now supported by John Lilburne's Eastern Association dragoons, and evidently those of the Northern Army under Col. Thomas Morgan, possibly backed by a division of horse, to deal with the Whitecoats, and with the remainder of his force by-passed them.

The 'last stand' of Newcastle's men in one report lasted for an hour, although this seems likely to be an exaggeration. But the fighting was bitter, though the end inevitable. The dragoons probably dismounted, and opened fire on the massed target of the Royalist hedgehog[29] 'to open them upon some hand, which at length they did; when all their ammunition was spent, having refused quarter, every man fell in the same order and rank wherein he had fought...'

The contemporary writer William Lilley, using as his authority Capt. Camby, 'Then a trooper under Cromwell', gives more details:[30]

[The Whitecoats] by mere valour, for one whole hour, kept the troops of horse from entering among them at near push of pike. When the horse did enter, they would have no quarter, but fought it out till there was not thirty of them living; those whose hap it was to be beaten down upon the ground as the troopers came to be near them, though they could not rise for their wounds, yet were so desperate as to get either a pike or sword or piece of them, and to gore the troopers' horses as they came over them, or passed by them... [Camby,] who was the third or fourth man that entered amongst them, protested he never in all the fights he was in, met with such resolute brave fellows, or whom he pitied so much, [and said] that he saved two or three against their wills.

It was said that Sir Thomas Fairfax attempted to end the slaughter, riding among the troopers, calling on them to 'spare your fellow countrymen.'

So fell 'the brave white coats foot that stood to the last man till they were murthered and destroyed.'

It is impossible now to tell just how many of the gallant Whitecoats survived. In 1660 six of the officers of Newcastle's regiment are known still to have been alive, compared with seventeen from John Hilton's similar-sized regiment.[31] This certainly suggests a heavy casualty rate, and Posthumous Kirton was among those killed, together perhaps with two other northern colonels, Sir William Lambton and Sir Charles Slingsby, who died in the battle.

How far the Whitecoats' stand succeeded in its aim is also unclear. But perhaps the fact that Henry Cheator's Cumbrian foot, who began the battle in this area of the field, were still a strong enough unit to be added as a reinforcement to the garrison of Bolton Castle on Rupert's return march to Lancashire may hint that their sacrifice was not entirely in vain.

74. A harquebusier, the standard cavalry trooper of Civil War armies.
This figure wears a 'pot' helmet with protective nasal bar, and a long riding coat.
The swivel belt on which his carbine was mounted is shown in detail (upper left).
Note the powder flask which the trooper also carries.

Whilst the Whitecoats fought and died, Cromwell was closing in to finish Goring's horse. The Parliamentarians, probably at least 3,000 strong, deployed on the same ground where Goring's horse had stood at the start of the battle. There are virtually no surviving accounts of the action which followed; it is unclear which side took the offensive, nor do we know how many troopers Goring succeeded in re-mustering for the final encounter. It does seem, however, that the engagement, whatever its length, was fiercely contested, with heavy losses for the Royalists.[32]

...the enemy [Goring] seeing us come on in such a gallant posture... left all thoughts of pursuit, and began to think that they must fight again for that victory which they thought had been already got. They marching down the Hill upon us, from our Carriages, so that they fought upon the same

75. John Lilburne (1614?–57). Before the war Lilburne earned the nickname
of 'Free-Born John' after refusing to take an oath demanded by the Star Chamber.
He joined the Parliamentarian forces in 1642, and took part in the storming of Lincoln
in October 1643. He became a lieutenant-colonel of dragoons in 1644.

ground, and with the same Front that our right wing had before stood to
receive our charge.

After a fight of uncertain, though probably brief, duration, the Royalists broke and
fled towards York. It is unlikely that Cromwell's exhausted cavalry were able to
launch a serious pursuit.

It must now have been about 10 p.m., and, apart perhaps from some mopping
up operations against isolated parties of Royalist foot, fighting was virtually at an
end. At around this time, the Earl of Manchester returned to the field having
rallied about 500 Allied horse. Robert Douglas, a Scots eyewitness, claimed credit
for this:[33]

> ...my Lord Manchester was fleeing with a number of Scots officers. God used
> me as ane instrument to move him to come back againe; for I was gathering
> men a mile from the place, and having some there he drew that way, and
> having a purpose to goe away and some of our officers, as Colonel Liell, was
> persuading him to goe away, but I exhorted him before many witnesses to goe

back to the field, and he was induced; we came back about 5 or 600 horse; he only of all the Generalls was in the field.

There were, however, still a considerable number of Royalist horse in the area, probably a mixture of Goring's and Byron's troopers, somewhere north of Four Lanes Meet, or in the hollow between the two ridges where the Allies had originally deployed. Sir Philip Monckton, having failed to find his own men, came across them: —[34]

> I retired over the Glen, where I saw a body of some two thousand horse that were broken. As I endeavoured to rally them I saw Sir John Hurry come galloping through the glen. I rid to him, and told him, that there was none in that great body of horse but knew either himself or me, and that if he would help me to put them in order, we might regain the field. He told me, broken horse would not fight, and galloped from me towards York. I returned to that body. By that it was night and [Sir Marmaduke Langdale] having had those bodies he commanded broken, came to me, and we staid in the field until twelve a clock at night, when Sir John Hurry came, by order of the Prince, to retire to York.

Despite what Monckton obviously thought, it is likely that Urry was correct in his opinion. It is highly unlikely that broken and fragmented horse could have achieved anything by this stage in the battle.

By midnight Rupert and Newcastle, both having lost touch with their men, were back in York, the roads and fields between the city and Marston Moor filled with fugitives, the wounded, the dying and the dead. For the Royalists the battle was lost, and with it, so it would prove, the north of England and ultimately the war.

8

AFTERMATH

First news of disaster was carried to York by the crowd of fugitives from the battlefield, many of them wounded, who tried to gain entry into the town. Among them was Sir Henry Slingsby, who remembered:[1]

> We came late to York which made a great confusion: for at the barr [Micklegate] none was suffer'd to come in but such as were of the town, so that the whole street was throng'd up to the barr with wound'd and lame people, which made a pitifull cry among them.

Prince Rupert had no such problems in gaining admission, and arrived in York between midnight and 1 a.m. on 3 July, joining Lord Eythin, who sent orders to those troops still on the moor, probably mainly the disorganised cavalry mentioned by Sir Philip Monckton, to retire on York.

The Marquis of Newcastle also got back into York sometime during the night, but does not seem to have met Rupert until the morning. The encounter, according to the Parliamentarian writer Simeon Ashe,[2] who probably had an account from eyewitnesses, led to 'warm wordes' between prince and marquis, 'after their Rout; they charging each other, with the cause thereof.'

There are several versions of the debate which followed. The Duchess of Newcastle provided a sanitised account of how her husband preferred to remember it:[3]

> That night my Lord remained in York, and having nothing left in his power to do his Majesty any further service in that kind; for he had neither ammunition, nor money to raise more forces, to keep either York, or any other towns that were yet in his Majesty's devotion, well knowing that those which were left could not hold out long, and being also loath to have aspersions cast upon him, that he did sell them to the enemy, in case he could not keep them, he took a resolution, and that justly and honourably, to forsake the kingdom; and to that end, went the next morning to the Prince, and acquainted him with his design, desiring his Highness would be pleased to give this true and

just report of him to his Majesty, that he had behaved himself like an honest man, a gentleman, and a loyal subject. Which request the Prince having granted, my Lord took his leave.

There are a number of problems with Newcastle's version of events, not least that, only a few hours after the end of the battle, it was uncertain just how many of the Royalist forces might still be rallied. Cholmley, however, had heard reports that Newcastle had decided before the battle to resign his commission afterwards, even if the Royalists won a victory.[4]

In the final conference between the three men, Eythin rightly vetoed an ill-considered plan by Rupert to draw out the remaining foot in York and offer battle again. With probably no more than about 1,500 men available in the three regiments in the city, it would have been certain disaster. Then Eythin asked the prince what he would do:[5] 'Sayes the Prince: "I will rally my men". Sayes Generall Kinge "Know ye what Lord Newcastle will do?" Sayes Lord Newcastle: "I will goe into Holland (looking upon all as lost)."'

It was thought that Eythin, playing upon Newcastle's fears of criticism by his enemies, and resentment at the loss of his army, was chiefly responsible for persuading the marquis to adopt this course.[6] Certainly it seems to have been a *volte face* from earlier in the morning, when according to one account, the marquis had agreed to attempt to reach the town of Newcastle, and there try to rally his scattered forces, Rupert joining him as soon as he had re-recruited his own foot.[7]

Rupert's *Diary* gives a succinct version of the final encounter:[8]

The Prince would have him endeavour to recruit his forces. No (sayes he [Newcastle]) I will not endure the laughter of the Court and King sayd he would go with him; and so they did...

Newcastle rode out of York the same day, heading for Scarborough, where he took ship for Hamburg. With him went not only Eythin, but a number of the senior officers of the Northern Army. The Earl of Clarendon, writing many years later, attempted to take a charitable view of Newcastle's actions:[9]

All that can be said for the Marquis is, that he was so utterly tired with a Condition and Employment so contrary to his Humour, Nature and Education, that he did not consider the meanes or the way, that would let him out of it, and free him forever from having more to do with it.

Rupert was less forbearing. Apparently learning more regarding the extent of Eythin's intrigues, he reportedly sent orders for his arrest on a charge of treason, but they only reached Scarborough after Newcastle and his party had already set sail.

In any event, it would be left to the prince to salvage what he could from the wreckage of Royalist hopes.

If the Allies had won a decisive victory, it was not apparent to them at the close of 2 July, nor were they in any state immediately to exploit it. Of the three army commanders, only the Earl of Manchester, who may never have actually quit the field, remained with the army that night, and, whatever his abilities as a general, did something to redeem himself by his concern for the soldiers: 'The Earle of Manchester, about eleven a clock that night, did ride about to the Souldiers praising them', and promising them food next morning.

According to Ashe, the troops were suffering considerable hardship:[10]

> They having drained the wells to the mud, were necessitated to drinke the water out of ditches, and out of places puddled with the horse feet. Yea, through the scarcity of Accomodation, very few of the Common Souldiers did eat above the quantity of a penny loafe from Tuesday till Saturday morning, and had no beere at all.

Lord Fairfax was in bed at his home at Cawood, whilst the Earl of Leven had ridden hard through the night to Leeds, and was still in bed at noon the next day:[11]

> ...being much wearied that of the battle, with ordering of his army, and now quite spent with his long journey in the night, had cast himself down upon a bed to rest, when this gentleman [Lt–Col. James Somerville] coming quietly into the room, he awoke, and hastily cries out 'Lieutenant-Colonel, what news?' – 'All is safe, may it please your excellencie, the parliament's armies have obtained a great victory,' and then delivers this letter. The general upon the hearing of this, knocked upon his breast, and says 'I would to God I had died upon the place...

Whilst Leven was making his rather shamed-face way back to resume command, it was left to Manchester, Sir Thomas Fairfax, Crawford and Cromwell to deal with matters on the battlefield. The sight which greeted them at dawn on 3 July was grim indeed. Thousands of dead and wounded had lain out on the moor throughout the night, many being stripped of their clothing, arms and valuables, and if still alive sometimes murdered, both by soldiers and by civilians bent on loot. Such surgeons as were available would have been overwhelmed.

Some of the more prominent casualties might be rescued by friends, or if dead, identified by comrades, or in the case of Royalists, by prisoners such as Sir Charles Lucas, who, tears streaming down his face, was taken round the battlefield. But very many wounded died in the open without receiving any medical care.

The Allies conscripted the local villagers to bury the dead in great grave pits, one of them traditionally in the White Syke Close area. They also carried out a rough body count, reaching a total of 4,500. Though the Allies only admitted to an improbable 300 dead of their own, it seems more likely that perhaps 1,500 of those buried were from the Allied armies and the remainder Royalist.[12]

Besides those found and buried on the field of battle, thousands more probably lay for days undiscovered in the surrounding fields and woods, where they had been cut

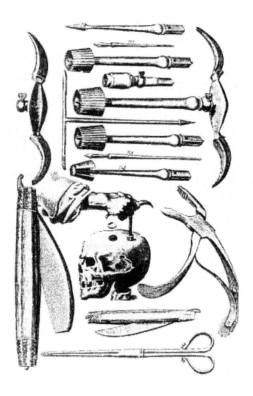

76. A surgeon's instruments, including a selection of drills used in 'trepanning' operations.

down in the pursuit, or had died from their wounds. All in all it may be that somewhere in the region of 8,000 men died either in the battle or soon afterwards.

Allied soldiers spent much of the day scouring the battlefield for abandoned arms and equipment. They collected about 10,000 arms of various kinds, as many as twenty-five guns, and at least forty barrels of powder. Also captured was Prince Rupert's 'sumpter' horse, carrying clothing and provisions. A particularly sad loss for the prince would have been his dog, Boye, whose body was found on the battlefield.

Among the prisoners was Rupert's major-general, Henry Tillier, and several commanders from the northern forces, who seem to have suffered the heaviest Royalist casualties. Seven of Newcastle's colonels were among the dead, and his foot was eliminated as an organised fighting force.

The Allies were initially almost as disorganised. A Royalist account claimed, probably with some exaggeration,[13]

Both armies were strangely scatter'd and confused of a sodaine. The enemy had not after the fight five hundred foote in a body, but of the Prince's horse there are not now a hundred wanting, but his foote suffered much, they standing soe stoutly to it, and the horse flying; most of Manchester's blew coats which fought under the bloody colours are cut off [probably Crawford's

77. Prince Rupert's dog, 'Boye'. Despite the rather strange shape of the animal portrayed here, 'Boye' was probably a large poodle, a breed used in the seventeenth century as hunting dogs.

regiment]. They have many colours of ours and we of theirs. More of the Enemye's slayne than of ours: more of ours taken than of theirs; but never were two such armyes soe sodainly and strangely scatter'd and soe few killed.

It took several days for accurate reports of the battle to reach London and Oxford. The first rumours spreading south spoke of a Royalist victory, so that celebration bonfires were lit in Pontefract and Newark, whilst the Royalist newspaper, *Mercurius Aulicus*, in its issue of 6 July proclaimed:[14]

But the great news of all is of what's done at Yorke... that the Rebels are absolutely routed, that the Prince with his Army hath taken 48 peece of Cannon, Generall Lesley and Sir Thomas Fairfax prisoners... The large Expresse from Prince Rupert's owne hand is (wee doubt not) before this with His Majestie.

Within two days the real story, at least in outline, was being published in London, where jubilation, for the Scots and Presbyterian faction at least, was somewhat modified by the major credit for the victory being claimed by Cromwell and the Independents.

At York, Rupert spent 3 July attempting to muster as many as possible of his scattered troops. Most of the surviving northern foot had disbanded themselves and headed for home, and his own infantry units were equally widely dispersed (some of

145

Sir Michael Ernley's officers ended up in Cumbria), though with time some would find their way back to their colours. For the present there was nothing the prince could do east of the Pennines, beyond appointing Sir Thomas Glemham to the somewhat empty position of colonel-general of the Northern Forces, and confirming George Goring in command of the Northern Horse. Most of the Royalist cavalry, and especially their mounts, were exhausted and in poor condition, and would take time to recover.

Early on 4 July,[15] 'the prince... marched out of [York via] Monkbar and so northwards towards Richmond... with the remaining horse, and as many of his footmen as he could force, leaving the rest in Yorke...'

He had with him about 3,500 horse and a few hundred foot, and halted at Richmond for two days to wait for more stragglers. Rupert was joined en route by Sir Robert Clavering with 1,300 horse from the northeast, and at Richmond met the Marquis of Montrose, pleading for assistance to launch his insurrection in Scotland. This the prince could no longer provide, and Montrose set off virtually alone on the first stages of his epic adventure.

Rupert had left Glemham to hold York with the 1,500 men of the three garrison regiments together with what support he could muster from the citizens and Royalist stragglers within the city, who were formed into several ad-hoc regiments for billeting and supply purposes. Morale was understandably low; Slingsby remembered:[16] 'Those that were left in York, out of hope of all relief, the town much distract'd and everyone ready to abandon hope.'

It was forty-eight hours before the Allies were ready to resume the siege, the Scots, according to one report, distinctly unenthusiastic at the prospect. On 4 July Glemham rejected their summons, trying to bolster the defenders' hopes by false reports of a victory by Prince Rupert. But he knew his situation to be hopeless. On 11 July he agreed to open negotiations with the besiegers.

Talks went on for several days. Largely through the intercession of Lord Fairfax, the Allies offered lenient terms, and on 16 July, the defenders of York, about 4,000 men in all, marched out, bound for the nearest Royalist garrison at Skipton.

Rupert had not kept his force of 5,000 horse together for long, as much perhaps because of difficulty in keeping them supplied as for other reasons. The Northern Horse were sent to Cumbria to refit and recruit, whilst Rupert and the remainder of his cavalry retreated across the Pennines into Lancashire. After spending several days hovering in north Lancashire, the prince, receiving news of the fall of York, retired to Chester, hoping to recruit his foot again in North Wales. Lord Byron was left at Liverpool to attempt the defence of Lancashire.

The Allied armies also did not stay together long after the capture of York. Differences between their commanders, always latent, became increasingly obvious. Lord Fairfax and his army was left to continue the slow business of reducing the remaining Royalist garrisons in Yorkshire. The Earl of Manchester, his subordinates Crawford and Cromwell already at odds with each other and the earl himself increasingly uneasy about the rise of the radical and Independent faction among the Parliamentarians, began to move slowly southwards through the Eastern Association.

78. James Graham, 5th Earl and 1st Marquis of Montrose (1612–50). One of the finest
commanders produced by the war, Montrose served with the Covenanters until 1640,
after which he became steadily disillusioned with the domination of the Scottish Parliament
by Argyle and the Prebyterian clergy. After the end of the Second Scots War
he gradually shifted his support to the King. In 1643 Montrose went to Oxford,
but not until the following year, when it would prove to be too late, did he receive
permission to launch a Royalist uprising in Scotland.

The Scots turned against the Royalist garrisons of Newcastle and Carlisle, which
would occupy their attention for many months to come.

There has been considerable debate on whether the defeat at Marston Moor
inevitably doomed the Royalist cause in the north of England. Certainly pockets of
resistance, in the shape of garrisons such as Carlisle, Scarborough, Pontefract,
Helmsley and Skipton, remained. Though some would be reduced in the course of
1644, others, including Carlisle and Pontefract, held out for over a year, until the
destruction of the last major Royalist field army at Naseby (June 1645) convinced
their defenders of the futility of further resistance. So long as they remained, the
possibility of a Royalist revival in the north could not be entirely discounted.

Royalist hopes of a recovery in the north would be greatly strengthened if they
could maintain their rather insecure presence in Lancashire. Prospects of this seemed
at first to have been improved by the enemy decision to break up the Army of Both
Kingdoms and send its contingents their separate ways, instead of crossing the
Pennines to complete the destruction of Rupert's forces. By dividing his own

79. Sir Marmaduke Langdale (1598–1661). A Yorkshireman, Langdale had opposed Charles I over the imposition of Ship Money, but rallied to the Royalist cause on the outbreak of war. A colonel in the Northern Army by 1643, Langdale would later gain a considerable reputation as an independent-minded but often effective commander during his leadership of the Northern Horse in 1644–45.

remaining troops, however, leaving north of the Mersey only Lord Byron with the survivors of Molyneux's brigade of horse, together with Tyldesley's foot and the Liverpool garrison, the prince greatly reduced the chances of prolonged resistance in Lancashire.

The task of dealing with Byron's forces was given to Sir John Meldrum, joined by the Lancashire Parliamentarian troops which had been sent reinforce the Allies before Marston Moor, and some excellent Cheshire foot, probably all musketeers, under Col. John Booth. His initial objective was to prevent the Royalists from recruiting in Lancashire and to drive out Molyneux's brigade of horse which provided the main field force available to Byron, who was severely hindered by lack of foot.

An added complication for the Parliamentarian commander was that Sir Marmaduke Langdale, who had taken over the Northern Horse when Goring was summoned south by the King to replace Lord Wilmot as lieutenant-general of the Oxford Army horse, was now moving south into Lancashire with 2,000–3,000 horse.[17]

Langdale's men, driving herds of plundered cattle along with them, terrified the civilian population of the Fylde area of Lancashire when they descended on them with all the impact of a Biblical plague of locusts: —[18]

> ...they ranged, some of them three or four myles from their quarters, to pilfer and plunder without respect to any persons, as well from their friends as Enemie... And wherever they saw any fat Cattell in any man's Closes or Sheepe they fetched them to their Quarters and killed them. They left not many pullen [poultry] where they saw them, as also young geese... They carried along with them many Strumpets, whom they termed 'Leaguer Ladies'. These they made use of in places where they lay; in a very uncivill and unbecoming way.

80. Dragoon and camp follower. Many women, some more respectable than others, followed the armies. The Northern Horse met with particular disapproval among the 'godly' because of the large numbers of 'leaguer ladies' who accompanied them.

Evading Meldrum near Preston, and crossing to the southern bank of the River Ribble, Langdale linked up with Molyneux, and the combined force of at least 3,000 horse and 200 foot halted for the night of 19 August on open moorland just to the south of the town of Ormskirk. They remained there throughout the next day, awaiting instructions from Byron at Liverpool, having evidently lost touch with Meldrum. At about 8 p.m. that evening, Byron arrived to consult with Molyneux and Langdale, admitting that:[19]

> I thought of nothing less than fighting that day, as having no intelligence of the enemyes being so neere, and came only from Leverpoole upon a pacing nagge [an ordinary riding horse not trained for battle] to advice with Sir Marmaduke on what was fitt to be done.

81. Sir Thomas Tyldesley (1596–1651). Arguably the driving force of the Lancashire Royalists, Tyldesley, a Roman Catholic, was knighted for gallantry at the storming of Burton-on-Trent (2 July 1643). After fighting at 1st Newbury, Tyldesley returned north with Byron. Later governor of Lichfield, he was killed at the Battle of Wigan Lane in 1651.

Unknown to the Royalists, Meldrum, with about 1,500 horse and a similar number of foot, was back on their trail and rapidly approaching Ormskirk from the north.

According to Byron, the Royalists were about to resume their march when:[20]

> ...we received the alarm we were ready to march away but seeing that the enemyes partye of horse was already entered the Towne we faced the enemy until most of our Horse retreated only left Lord Molyneux his brigade which was some 1400 horse and some dragoons [probably Tyldesley's foot] to make the retreat good, it being his course to bringe up the reare. The enemy came fast on, and the Moore was straite, so that they, with the helpe of their horse and foote forced them to retreat to another Moore where the rest of our Horse were drawne upp in good order ready to receive them.

From this point Royalist resistance rapidly fell apart. There was much mutual recrimination among the Royalist commanders involved, but it seems that Tyldesley's foot were unable to withstand Booth's musketeers for the good reason that they had fired off most of their ammunition at Marston Moor and not yet had it replenished. Langdale was never a good subordinate, described by Clarendon as:[21] 'a man hard to please, and of very weak understanding, yet proud, and much in love with his own judgement.'

He was probably by now working to his own agenda, and the outcome was that the Northern Horse, whose morale was in any case very low, apparently quit the field leaving Byron and Molyneux to their fate. Molyneux's horse, left unsupported, broke and fled[22] 'in such a terror... that they would not be stopped till they came to Leverpool.'

Many of Tyldesley's foot were hunted down, whilst according to the Parliamentarians, Byron and Molyneux only escaped by hiding in a cornfield.

The defeat at Ormskirk cost the Royalists about 300 men and 800–1,000 horses. It also ended any hope of their making a sustained stand in Lancashire. Langdale and his horse, rejecting all Byron's pleas to remain with him, headed south on the first stage of an eventful march to link up with the King. Evidently despairing of rebuilding his army when his new North Wales levies deserted almost as quickly as they were conscripted, Rupert himself also now left the area, establishing his new headquarters at Bristol.

Faced, as he had predicted in the event of defeat even before the start of the York march, with a resurgence of Parliamentarian activity threatening the insecure Royalist position on the Welsh Marches, Byron collected most of his remaining troops together in an attempt to recapture the key garrison of Montgomery Castle, recently secured by the Parliamentarians. On 18 September, however, he suffered another serious reverse, in which despite the strong showing of the remaining foot from Ireland, the Royalist horse once again failed to distinguish themselves.

It was the end of the last effective Royalist field army in the north. Freed from the danger of any relief attempt, Meldrum turned his attention to Liverpool, which surrendered early in November following a mutiny by troops from Ireland in its

82. A 'firelock'. So called from the type of musket with which he is armed.
This has a flintlock, and, not requiring a match to fire it, was slightly more reliable in wet
and windy weather. This soldier carries his ammunition in a powder bag slung across
his shoulders.

garrison. Lathom House, strategically irrelevant, maintained a hopeless resistance for
another year, whilst Byron, displaying all his formidable powers of determination and
resourcefulness, held on at Chester until February 1646.

Marston Moor has a strong claim to be regarded as the decisive battle of the First
Civil War. A Royalist victory there, even if incomplete, would not only have
preserved York for the King, but almost certainly have led to the break-up of the
fragile Allied Army of Both Kingdoms. Recriminations between English and Scots,
the latter about to be faced by the Royalist rising orchestrated by Montrose, perhaps
strengthened by military assistance from a victorious Rupert, would have been bitter,
and probably have led to the withdrawal of the remaining Scots forces from England,
leaving the northeast to pass once more into Royalist hands almost by default. Lord
Fairfax would have been faced once again with defending his heartland in the West
Riding, this time perhaps against the combined forces of Rupert and Newcastle. If
the Royalist situation in the south had permitted it, the prince would no doubt have
completed his conquest of northwest England by reducing Manchester.

The Parliamentarian Army of the Eastern Association would have been forced to concentrate its attention on defending its home territories against enemy incursions, and an already reluctant Earl of Manchester would have been even less willing to commit his troops in support of the southern Parliamentarian armies of Essex and Waller. Already battered by the King during the summer campaign, these might have disintegrated before winter. Faced with such large-scale defeat, the Independent 'war party', and their military champion Cromwell, perhaps discredited by the failure of the Scots alliance and disaster at Marston Moor, might well have lost their uneasy control at Westminster. It is not hard to imagine, given a modicum of political wisdom by the King (perhaps an unlikely eventuality) a compromise peace early in 1645 with the more moderate elements in the Parliamentary party, or renewed fighting in the spring with the Royalists having a clear military superiority.

These are, of course, the 'what ifs' of 'alternative' history. It is perhaps more rewarding to attempt to strike a balance sheet of the successes and failures of the 1644 campaign in the north as it was actually fought.

First the defeated, and here the figure of Prince Rupert dominates history as he did the events of the campaign.

The prince had three distinct objectives in 1644, each of which, ideally, should have been completed in its turn before embarking upon the next. His first task, in

83. Lord Molyneux commanded Byron's second line at Marston Moor.
The horned moon, and the motto: 'But if I shine alas for my horn', was a jibe at the
Parliamentarian Earl of Essex, who had been cuckolded by his wife.

the spring, was to rebuild the Royalist position on the Welsh Border and West Midlands, thrown into jeopardy by Byron's defeat at Nantwich. In this Rupert had undeniable success, reforming the inefficient administrative and command structure of the area, and rebuilding the Royalist field army. He also effectively saw off Meldrum's unexpected threat to Newark.

However, as Byron for one perceived, Rupert's success stood upon very insecure foundations. He failed, for example, to take key Parliamentarian garrisons such as Nantwich and Wem, nor was he able to leave behind sufficient troops to maintain Royalist control. Even before Marston Moor, the Royalists on the Welsh Border had begun to lose ground to Denbigh's Parliamentarian forces. Rupert could have claimed with some justification that this situation was not of his making. The pressure he came under from Newcastle, and to a lesser extent from the Lancashire Royalist leadership, to begin his operations in the north as quickly as possible played a part. Indirectly, Rupert was also pushed into acting earlier than he would have wished by his well-founded fears that the King and his advisers would abandon the agreed strategy in the south.

Similar factors were at work in the Lancashire campaign. This is often seen as a mere prelude to the famous 'Yorke March', but it was intended as a major operation in its own right. Certainly Liverpool was named as the major objective in Royalist correspondence prior to the campaign, but there are hints that Rupert's aims may have gone beyond this, certainly as far as taking Manchester and consolidating Royalist control of the county. He may even have toyed with the idea of sending Montrose, with a viable force of troops, on a thrust into the western lowlands of Scotland. Once again, however, events elsewhere forced his hand. Unfortunately, several letters which passed between King Charles and the prince in the earlier stages of the campaign have evidently not survived, but the famous instructions of 14 June from the King, quoted earlier, were emphatic in their command that, 'all other designs laid aside', he should give absolute priority to the relief of York. The result was, as on the Welsh Border, that Royalist success in Lancashire remained half completed.

The 'Yorke March' is rightly regarded as one of Rupert's finest achievements. The Allies were completely out-manoeuvred and baffled, and York triumphantly relieved on 1 July without a blow being struck.

But if Rupert's plans since leaving Lancashire had hitherto gone without a hitch, henceforward his sureness of touch totally deserted him. The Marquis of Newcastle had a major part to play in this, and the actions of the two principal Royalist commanders, with Lord Eythin as a possibly malign background influence, have to be considered together.

Newcastle's showing in the 1644 campaign in the north so far had been unremarkable. Although admittedly seriously outnumbered by the Scots foot, he had failed to capitalise on his cavalry superiority, and indeed the latter had suffered severely through undue exposure to wintry conditions. Although Newcastle and Eythin could claim to have delayed the Scots advance, they had not been able to bring them to decisive action when time was of the essence. Caution had always been

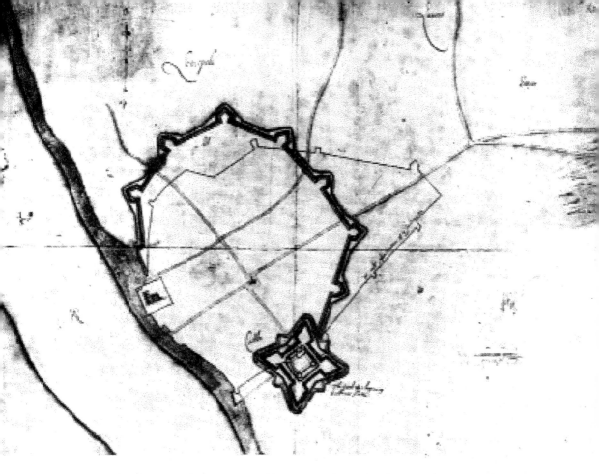

84. Plan by Bernard De Gomme of his proposed new fortifications for Liverpool after its capture by the Royalists in 1644. It is unclear how far these were completed before the Parliamentarians laid siege to the town later in the year.

the hallmark of Eythin's military philosophy, and it was never more in evidence than during the 1644 campaign.

It was, however, in their relationship, or lack thereof, in the hours leading up to Marston Moor that Rupert, Newcastle and Eythin are most open to condemnation. Part of the blame must lie in King Charles' failure to establish a clear command hierarchy for after the Royalist armies met, but neither Rupert nor Newcastle seem to have made any real attempt to resolve the situation. In effect Newcastle sulkily acquiesced in Rupert's assumption of command, whilst, incited by Eythin, taking every opportunity to obstruct and drag his heels. Both Newcastle and Eythin, with some supporting grounds, were bitterly opposed to the prince's strategy of bringing the Allies to immediate battle, and Eythin was certainly also motivated by his personal animosity towards Rupert.

Rupert, for his part, lacked the tact and patience necessary in dealing with someone of Newcastle's delicate sensibilities. Even his own officers had recently complained of the prince's tendency not to share his plans with them. By treating Newcastle as though he were a recalcitrant junior officer whose role was to obey orders without discussion, Rupert threw away any real possibility of obtaining his

85. Pontefract town and castle. A strategically important garrison which withstood a long siege before falling to the Parliamentarians in July 1645.

support and co-operation. Indeed he also threw away his only real chance of victory.

So far as events on 2 July are concerned, it is tempting to think that Rupert lost a valuable opportunity by his failure to launch a major attack whilst the Allies were still returning from their Wetherby march and forming up on the ridge overlooking Marston Moor. But, whatever his other faults, Rupert was never lacking in aggressive spirit, and it is probably reasonable to assume that he would have attacked had it been practicable.

The prince's final and greatest error was in assuming in the early evening that the Allies would not attack that day, and ordering a partial stand-down of his forces. Again, frustration with Newcastle and Eythin may have played a part, together with a lack of full information on enemy deployment. But Rupert had made the fatal error of underestimating his opponent, and would pay dearly for it.

There is little to say regarding Rupert and Newcastle's role in the actual battle. Neither ever got to grips with the situation in the way a general might be expected to have done. Displays of personal gallantry were not enough. Of their subordinates, the honours of the day must rest with George Goring. He displayed his customary quick thinking in an emergency, disposed of Fairfax, and came near to breaking the Allied foot. His eventual rout by Cromwell was more the result of a disparity in numbers than of any error.

Lord John Byron had always been a capable cavalry commander, and, although Rupert by implication made him one of the principal scapegoats for the Royalist defeat, evidence is insufficient to support such a conclusion. Heavily outnumbered, Byron in fact put up tough and prolonged resistance to Cromwell and Leslie, before being overwhelmed. Unfortunately Byron, a prolific writer on his experiences, seems to have left no account of Marston Moor, beyond a brief reference in a letter to Ormonde to the defeat being the result of 'Such gross errors as I have not patience to describe'. Certainly during the coming months he would become steadily more disillusioned with Prince Rupert.

Not enough is known of the actions of any of the Royalist infantry commanders to form a judgement on their performance. Whoever led Newcastle's foot performed creditably, and it is tempting to think that Eythin may, at least in part, have atoned for his earlier failings.

On the Allied side Alexander Leslie, Earl of Leven, deserves more credit than he is sometimes given. His campaign against Newcastle was a considerable achievement. Although he failed to capture the port of Newcastle-upon-Tyne, Leven, hindered as he was by the inexperience of many of his foot, his inferior cavalry, and the long and insecure lines of communication, managed to out-manoeuvre Newcastle, avoid battle in unfavourable circumstances, and preserve the bulk of his army intact until he could link up with his English allies.

On 2 July it was apparently Leven who saw the opportunity which presented itself in the evening, and persuaded his colleagues to attack. It was an uncharacteristically bold action by one normally regarded as ultra-cautious, and it paid rich dividends. Unfortunately Leven would later lose some credit for allowing himself to be persuaded to leave the field, believing the battle lost. None regretted it more than the earl himself.

Neither Lord Fairfax nor the Earl of Manchester had any cause for self-congratulation on their performance, though Manchester did at least return to the field at the end of the day. The laurels of victory rested with their subordinates.

The role of Sir Thomas Fairfax has sometimes been exaggerated. In fact it is hard to discern any contribution made by him to the Allied victory. Though admittedly facing a very difficult task, the cavalry under his command were thoroughly beaten, and Sir Thomas's subsequent personal adventures, though colourful, had little bearing on events.

Main credit for the Allied victory must rest with Oliver Cromwell, David Leslie and Lawrence Crawford. Unfortunately personal, political and religious animosity between the three men and their supporters has clouded and confused the exact share of each in the victory. It may be, in fact, that, for their key actions at different vital points of the battle, all three deserve equal praise.

86. Rupert's dog, 'Boye', had been demonised in Parliamentarian propaganda since the start of the war, and was credited with supernatural powers. His death at Marston Moor was a subject of great celebration in Parliamentarian newssheets. Here Rupert, with asses ears, and dressed as a priest, is presiding over the dog's burial.

The effects of Marston Moor spread like ripples for the remainder of the war. It has been argued that, given generalship of even average ability, the now greatly superior resources of the Allies could have brought about the defeat of the King by the end of 1644. In the event, the Scots were tied down by lengthy sieges of Newcastle and Carlisle, and disputes with their English allies over the payment of their promised subsidies. It would not be until the late summer of 1645, when the war was already effectively won, that they would make an incursion in strength into the English Midlands.

Though Lord Fairfax remained preoccupied with reducing the remaining Royalist garrisons in the north, and guarding against any resurgence by the King's supporters there, Marston Moor in theory released the powerful Army of the Eastern

Association for use elsewhere. But the growing divisions between the Presbyterian and Independent factions in its own leadership, and Manchester's own increasing doubts about political developments, largely negated its effectiveness. The King was able to avoid destruction at the Second Battle of Newbury (20 October) largely because of divisions among his opponents, and lived to fight another day.

The huge political boost given to the Independents by the victory at Marston Moor greatly increased their influence at Westminster, however, and, coupled with anger after the King's escape at Newbury, enabled them to push through the legislation needed for the formation of the ultimately war-winning New Model Army.

For the Royalists, the defeat at Marston Moor meant the loss of the resources in supplies and manpower of the north of England, as well as the destruction of their second-largest field army. Henceforward the King would face crippling odds, and, barring the totally unexpected, an ultimately hopeless fight for survival. Prince Rupert, though probably suffering a major personal crisis of confidence following his defeat, did not lose the support of his uncle, and in November was made effective commander-in-chief of the Royalist armies. In this position personal failings already displayed at Marston Moor would be even more evident, though to give him credit, Rupert himself seems to have hoped to achieve no more than military stalemate.

For the remainder of the war, the hope of a Royalist revival in the north, boosted by such episodes as Sir Marmaduke Langdale's successful relief of Pontefract in March 1645, was a key factor in the King's strategy. Rupert's desire to avenge Marston Moor, and re-establish a Royalist presence in the north, was an important consideration in planning the spring 1645 campaign, and the tensions and disagreements it aroused among the Royalist leadership a major cause of their decisive defeat on the field of Naseby, a battle which was itself a direct consequence of the events almost twelve months earlier on Marston Moor.

APPENDIX

ORDERS OF BATTLE
2 JULY 1644

Partly because of the nature of surviving contemporary sources, it is virtually impossible to compile an entirely definitive Order of Battle of Royalist units present at Marston Moor. This is especially true of the Marquis of Newcastle's Northern Army. The units listed here, however, were all almost certainly present, although the tally may not be complete.

PRINCE RUPERT'S ARMY

General:	Prince Rupert (also *de facto* Royalist commander-in-chief)
General and lieutenant-general of horse:	vacant
Field-marshal-general:	John, Lord Byron
Major-general of foot:	Henry Tillier (Sir Thomas Tyldesley may have been major-general of the Lancashire forces)
General of ordnance:	unknown

Horse

Right Wing:

Commander:	John, Lord Byron
First line:	(Sgt-Maj.-Gen. Sir John Urry)
Sir John Urry's regiment:	200 men, Oxford Army (raised 1643, at Chalgrove, High Wycombe, First Newbury and Newark)
Sir William Vaughan's regiment:	300 men (formed late 1643 from English troops in Ireland, at Newark)

Lord Byron's regiment:	300 men, Oxford Army (raised 1642, Edgehill, Burford, Roundway Down, First Newbury, Nantwich)
Marcus Trevor's regiment:	400 men, Welsh Marches army (raised 1642/3, Middlewich 1643, Nantwich)

Detached:

Samuel Tuke's regiment:	200 men, Northern/Newark Horse (raised 1642/43 as Duke of York's regiment, Lincolnshire campaign, 1643, Newark 1644)
Second Line:	(Richard, Lord Molyneux)
Lord Molyneux's regiment:	300 men, Oxford Army (raised 1642/3, Lancashire, First Newbury, Nantwich)
Sir Thomas Tyldesley's regiment:	300 men (raised 1642, Lancashire, Burton-on-Trent, First Newbury, Nantwich)
Thomas Leveson's regiment:	200 men, Dudley Castle Garrison (raised 1643, Newark)
Prince Rupert's regiment:	500 men, Oxford Army (raised 1642, Powick Bridge, Edgehill, Chalgrove, First Newbury, Newark)

Reserve:

Prince Rupert's lifeguard:	150 men, Oxford Army (raised 1642, Powick Bridge, Edgehill, Chalgrove, Bristol, First Newbury, Market Drayton, Newark)

Dragoons

Henry Washington's regiment:	500 men, Oxford Army (Edgehill, Lichfield, Bristol, First Newbury, Lancashire Campaign)

Foot

Major-general Henry Tillier

Henry Warren's regiment:	500 men, Army of Leinster (raised 1640 as Lord Lieutenant's regiment, Middlewich, Nantwich)
Sir Thomas Tyldesley's regiment:	1,000 men, Oxford Army (raised 1642, Lancashire, Burton-on-Trent, First Newbury, Lancashire Campaign)
Sir Michael Earnley /Richard Gibson's regiments:	500 men, Army of Leinster (brigaded together after their heavy losses at Nantwich) (both raised 1640, Middlewich, Nantwich)
Robert Broughton's regiment:	1,000 men, Army of Leinster (raised North Wales, 1640, Newark, Lancashire Campaign)

Henry Tillier's regiment:	1,000 men, Army of Leinster (formed 1643 from detachments from a number of regiments, Newark, Lancashire Campaign)
Lord Byron's regiment:	500 men (raised 1644, included a number of 'native Irish' troops, Welsh Border, Lancashire Campaign)
Prince Rupert's regiment:	1,000 men, Oxford Army (raised 1642, Edgehill, Chalgrove, Bristol, First Newbury, Lancashire Campaign)
Henry Cheator's Regiment:	1,000 men, Bolton Castle Garrison, possibly included troops from Ireland
Edward Chisenall's regiment:	1,000 men (raised May/June 1644, partly from Lathom House garrison)
Derbyshire Foot:	500 men (combined regiments of John Millward, John Frescheville and Rowland Eyre)

NORTHERN ARMY

General:	Marquis of Newcastle
Lieutenant-general:	Lord Eythin
General of horse:	Lord George Goring
Lieutenant-general of horse:	Sir Charles Lucas
Major-general of foot:	Sir Francis Mackworth

Horse

It is impossible to compile a definitive list of all of the regiments present at Marston Moor. A large number of, in many cases very weak, units were organised into probably seven brigades, commanded by Sir William Blakiston, Sir Marmaduke Langdale, Richard Dacre, Francis Carnaby, Sir Charles Lucas, Lord Widdrington and the Newark Horse, the latter probably commanded by Sir John Mayney or Rowland Eyre. Unless stated otherwise, all units served with Newcastle's forces throughout the 1643 and 1644 campaigns.

Regiments

Sir Francis Anderson:	raised 1642, Northumberland
Sir William Blakiston:	raised 1643, Durham and Yorkshire
Sir William Bradshaw:	raised 1642/3, Lancashire
Robert Brandling:	raised 1643/4, Northumberland and Durham
Francis Carnaby:	raised 1642/3, Northumberland
Lord Henry Cavendish:	raised 1643, Yorkshire
Sir Richard Dacre:	raised 1643, Yorkshire
Sir Robert Dallison:	raised 1643, Lincolnshire (Newark Horse)

Sir Gameliel Dudley:	raised 1643, Yorkshire
William Eure:	raised 1642/3, Yorkshire and Durham (served with Oxford Army at First Newbury, returned north with Sir Charles Lucas)
Lord Eythin:	raised 1643, Yorkshire (included some Scots)
John Fenwick:	raised 1643, Northumberland
Sir John Girlington:	raised 1643, Lancashire and Yorkshire
Sir Thomas Glemham:	raised 1642, Yorkshire
Sir Francis Howard:	raised 1642, Northumberland
Sir John Key:	raised 1642, Yorkshire
Sir Marmaduke Langdale:	raised 1642/3, Yorkshire
Sir Ferdinando Leigh:	raised 1643, Yorkshire
Sir Charles Lucas:	raised 1643, Yorkshire and Lincolnshire (served with Oxford Army at First Newbury)
Sir Francis Mackworth:	raised Lincolnshire, 1643
Francis Malham:	raised 1643?, Yorkshire
Lord Mansfield:	raised 1642, Yorkshire
Sir William Mason:	raised 1643, Yorkshire
Sir Thomas Metham (Newcastle's lifeguard):	possibly formed just before the battle
Sir George Middleton:	raised 1643, Lancashire
Sir Philip Monckton:	raised Yorkshire, 1643
Ralph Mylott:	raised 1642, Durham, Northumberland and Yorkshire
Sir William Pelham:	raised 1643, Lincolnshire, (Newark Horse)
George Porter:	raised 1643, Midlands (lifeguard, one troop)
Sir John Preston:	raised 1643, Northumberland and Yorkshire
John Belasyse (ex-Sir William Saville):	raised 1642, Yorkshire
Thomas Slingsby:	raised 1643, Yorkshire
Francis Stuart:	raised 1643? (small Scots unit)
Sir Richard Tempest:	raised 1643, Durham, Northumberland and Yorkshire
Sir Walter Vavasour:	raised 1642, Yorkshire
Lord Widdrington:	raised 1642, Northumberland and Durham
Sir Edward Widdrington:	raised 1642, Northumberland and Durham

Foot

The same provisos apply as when discussing the northern cavalry. A large number of mostly very weak regiments seem to have formed five divisions, each about 500–800 strong. One or two regiments, such as Newcastle's and Sir William Lambton's, may still have been strong enough to form a full division.

Anthony Byerley ('Byerley's Bulldogs'):	raised 1643/4, Durham
Sir Phillip Byron:	a very small obscure unit, which may have included troops from Ireland

Cuthbert Conyers:	raised 1643, Durham
Lord Eythin:	raised 1643, mixed northern unit
Sir Timothy Fetherstonhaugh:	raised 1643, Yorkshire
Godfrey Floyd:	raised 1643, Yorkshire
Thomas Forster:	raised 1643, Northumberland
Sir John Girlington:	raised 1643, Lancashire
John Hilton:	raised 1642, Durham ('Whitecoats')
Sir William Huddlestone:	raised 1642, Cumbria
Sir Richard Hutton:	raised 1642, Yorkshire
Richard Kirkebride:	raised 1643, Cumbria
Sir William Lambton:	raised 1642, Durham ('Whitecoats'). One of units involved in 'last stand', Lambton killed
John Lamplugh:	raised 1643, Cumbria
Sir Marmaduke Langdale:	raised 1643, Yorkshire
Sir Francis Mackworth:	raised 1642, Yorkshire and Lincolnshire
Lord Mansfield:	raised late 1643, Derbyshire
Marquis of Newcastle (Col. Posthumous Kirton):	raised 1642, Northumberland ('Whitecoats'), involved in 'last stand', Kirton killed
Charles Slingsby:	raised 1643?, Northumberland
John Tempest:	raised 1644, Durham
Sir Richard Tempest:	raised 1644, Durham
Lord Widdrington:	raised 1642/3, Northumberland, Durham and Yorkshire

Dragoons

Sir Gameliel Dudley:	raised 1642, Yorkshire
Sir Marmaduke Langdale:	raised 1642, Yorkshire

William Prideaux ('a very valiant man, and slew 14 or 16 of the Rebels with his own hand at Marston Moor'), killed

ALLIED ARMIES

Commander-in-chief:	Earl of Leven

ARMY OF THE EASTERN ASSOCIATION

General:	Earl of Manchester
Lieutenant-general of horse:	Oliver Cromwell
Major-general of foot:	Lawrence Crawford

Horse

Earl of Manchester:	11 troops (*c.*700 men)
Oliver Cromwell:	14 troops (*c.*800 men)
Charles Fleetwood:	6 troops (*c.*400 men)
Bartholomew Vermuyden:	5 troops (*c.*350 men)

Dragoons

John Lilburne

Foot

	Strength	
	May 1644	23 July 1644
Earl of Manchester:	1628	1053
Lawrence Crawford:	850	608
John Pickering:	738	524
Sir Miles Hobart:	883	593 (August)
Edward Montagu:	759	418
Francis Russell:	932	662

ARMY OF THE NORTHERN ASSOCIATION

General:	Ferdinando, Lord Fairfax
Lieutenant-general of horse:	Sir Thomas Fairfax

Horse

Sir Thomas Fairfax
John Lambert
Charles Fairfax
Hugh Bethell
Ferdinando, Lord Fairfax
Sir William Constable
Sir William Fairfax
Sir Thomas Norcliffe
Christopher Copley

Dragoons

Thomas Morgan

Foot

John Bright
Sir William Fairfax (Lt-Col. Simon Needham)
Sir William Constable (Lt-Col. William Forbes)
Lord Fairfax
George Dodding (Lancashire troops)

ARMY OF THE SOLEMN LEAGUE AND COVENANT

General: Alexander Leslie, Earl of Leven
Lieutenant-general of horse: David Leslie
Major-generals of foot: William Baillie, Sir James Lumsden
General of artillery: Sir Alexander Hamilton

Horse

Each regiment *c*.300–350 men

Earl of Leven (Lord Balgonie)
Earl of Dalhousie
Earl of Eglinton
David Leslie
Earl of Balcarres
Lord Kirkudbright

Dragoons

Hugh Frazer (*c*.600 men)

Foot

Each regiment *c*.800 men

William Douglas of Kilhead (Nithsdale and Annandale)
Earl of Cassilis (Kyle and Carrick)
Earl of Dunfermline (Fifeshire)
Lord Couper (Strathearn)
Earl of Buccleugh (Tweedale)
Earl of Loudon (Loudon and Glasgow)
Earl of Crawford-Lyndsey (Fifeshire)
Earl of Lauderdale (Midlothian)
Sir Alexander Hamilton (Clydesdale)

James Rae (Edinburgh)

Sir Arthur Erskine (Minister's regiment)

Sir Alexander Gibson (College of Justice regiment)

Lord Gordon (Sir James Lumsden) (Aberdeenshire)

Lord Livingston (Stirlingshire)

Lord Sinclair (Levied Regiment)

Master of Yester (Linlithgow and Tweedale)

MAPS AND PLANS OF BATTLE

Map 1. Location map of the battle for the north.

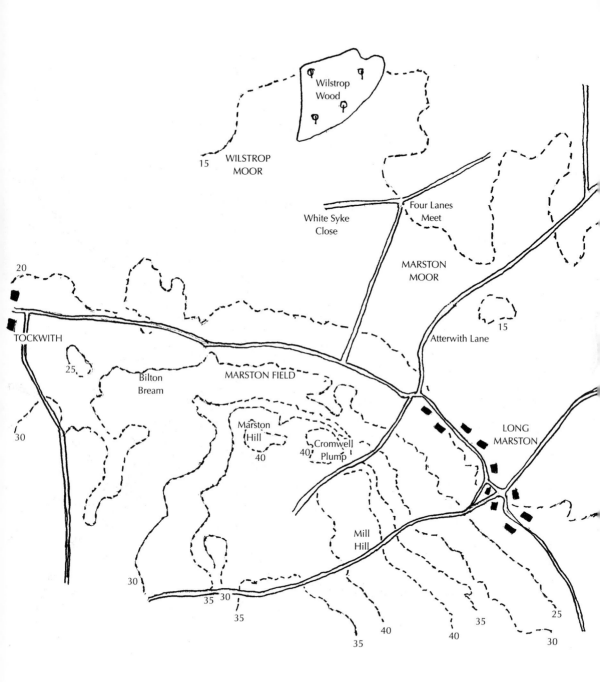

Map 2. Map of the battlefield.

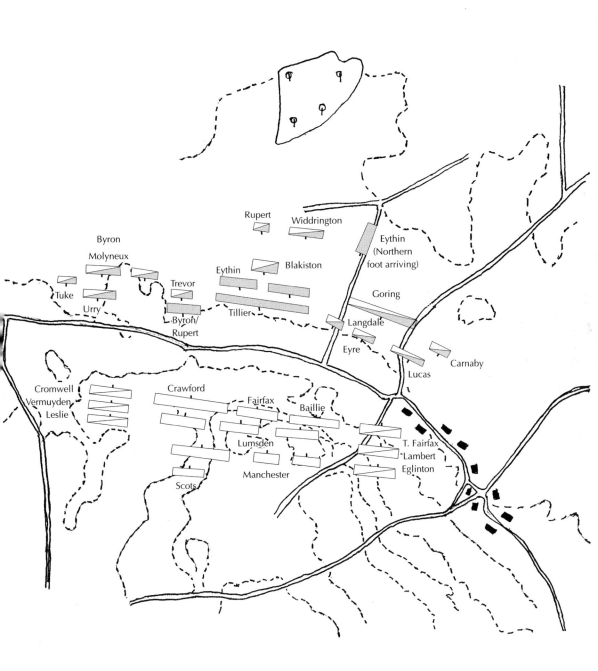

Map 3. Marston Moor Phase 1.

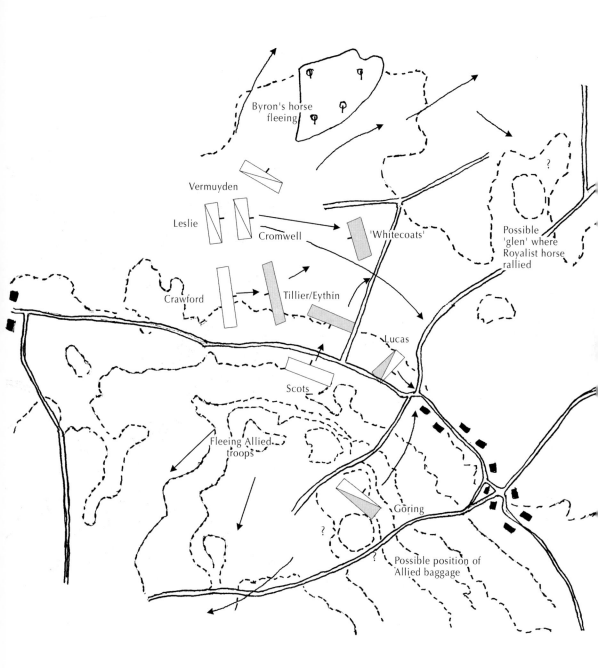

Map 4. Marston Moor Phase 2.

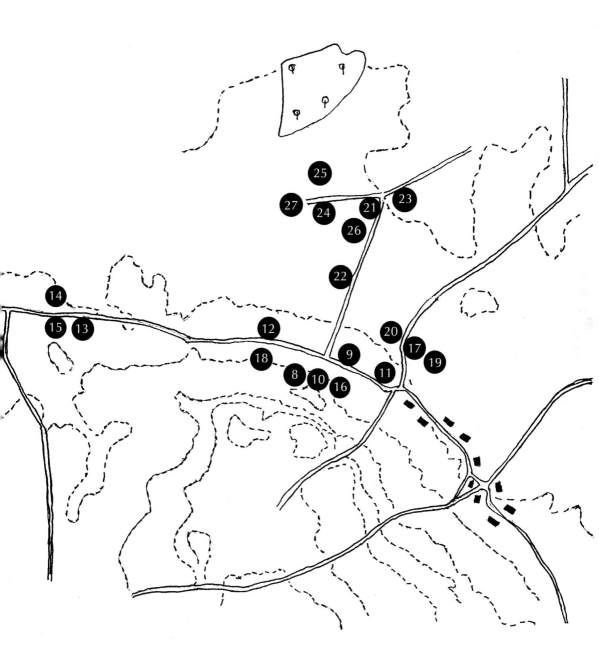

Map 5. Photograph locations.

NOTES

Chapter 1

1 C.V. Wedgwood, *The King's War*, London, 1957, pp.186–87.

2 D. Laing (ed.), *The Letters and Journals of Robert Baillie*, Edinburgh, 1842, ii, p.88.

3 Wedgwood, *op. cit.*, p.256.

4 Baillie, *op. cit.*, ii, p.100.

5 S.R. Gardiner, *History of the Great Civil War*, London, 1893, vol. 1, pp.231–32.

6 Baillie, *op. cit.*, I, p.218.

7 E.M. Furgol, *Regimental History of the Covenanting Armies*, Edinburgh, 1990, pp.2–3; S. Reid, *Scots Armies of the English Civil War*, Oxford, 1999, p.10.

8 S. Reid, *Scots Armies of the 17th Century*, Southend-on-Sea, 1990, I, p.7.

9 J.K. Gilbert, *History of the Irish Confederacy*, Dublin 1879, ii, p.266.

10 I. Ryder, *An English Army for Ireland*, Southend-on-Sea, 1989, *passim*; J. Barratt, *'Cure for the Scots': Troops from Ireland and the Royalist War Effort*, in *English Civil War Times*, No. 54, p.19.

11 For example, J.L. Malcolm, *'All the King's Men': the Impact of the Crown's Irish Soldiers in the English Civil War*, in *Irish Historical Studies*, vol. XXI, No. 83, 1979, pp.239–64.

12 Barratt, *op. cit.*, and Ryder, pp.23–24.

13 R. Hopton, *Bellum Civile*, Taunton, 1902 ed., p.62.

14 Ryder, *op. cit.*, pp.31–32.

15 T. Carte, *Life of Ormonde*, London, 1739, V, p.521.

16 *Ibid*, pp.504, 527.

17 *Ibid*, pp.505–06; Earl of Clarendon, *History of the Great Rebellion*, Oxford, 1888, III, p.35.

18 Carte, V, p.51.

19 *Ibid*, pp.505–06.

20 Gilbert, *op. cit.*, p.270.

21 Ryder, *op. cit.*, p.31.

22 E. Warburton, *Memoirs of Prince Rupert and the Cavaliers*, London, 1849, II, pp.327, 328, 330.

23 R. Hutton, *The Royalist War Effort*, London, 1982, pp.123–24.

24 Ryder, pp.31–32.

25 Historical Manuscripts Commission, *Report XX*, Appendix XI, p.41.

26 Chester Record Office, *AF/26/4*.

27 Chester Record Office, *Assembly Book*, f.64.

28 J. Barratt, *Civil War Stronghold*, Birkenhead, 1993, pp.3–5.

29 *Mercurius Civicus*, E.30.7.

30 J. Lowe, *Campaign of the Irish-Royalist Army in Cheshire*, in *Transactions of the Historic Society of Lancashire and Cheshire*, vol. 111, 1959, pp.60–61.

31 Lowe, *op. cit.*, pp.64–66.

32 Thomas, Lord Fairfax, *Brief Memorials...*, London, 1985 ed., p.37.

33 Byron to Prince Rupert, 14 January 1644, *B.L. Additional MS 18981, f.8*.

34 J. Barratt, *The Battle of Nantwich 1644*, Bristol, 1993, p.7.

35 Fairfax, *op. cit*, p.25.

36 *Ibid*. p.46.

37 E.W. Ives, *Drums Along the Weaver*, in *Cheshire*

Round, 1962, p.163.

38 J. Barratt, *Nantwich*, pp.8–20.

39 Quoted in Gardiner, *Great Civil War*, I, p.296; see also J. Barratt, *Cavaliers*, Stroud, 2000, pp.138–40.

Chapter 2

1   Sir Phillip Warwick, *Memoirs of the Reign of Charles I*, Edinburgh, 1825, p.235.

2   Barratt, *Cavaliers*, op.cit., pp.121–23.

3   Sir James Turner, *Memoirs*, ed. J. Thomson, Edinburgh, 1829, p.45.

4   Barratt, *op. cit.*, pp.126–27.

5   Quoted P.R. Newman, *The Old Service*, p.215.

6   Warwick, *op. cit.*, p.265.

7   *C.S.P.D.* 1644, p.31.

8   Stuart Reid, *All the King's Armies*, Staplehurst, 1998, pp.108–09.

9   Newcastle to Rupert, 28 January 1644, quoted Warburton, *op. cit.*, II, p.368.

10 Vicars, *Historical Collections*, II, pp.140–41.

11 Turner, *op. cit.*, p.29.

12 Newcastle and Eythin to King Charles, 13 February 1644, quoted Warburton, *op. cit.*, II, pp.483–84.

13 Reid, *All the King's Armies*, pp.110–11.

14 *Late Proceedings of the Scots Armie* E.E.2.31.

15 Firth, pp.200–01.

16 D. Appleby, *Our Fall Our Fame*, Newtown, 1996, p.80.

17 Turner, *op. cit.*, p.30.

18 Firth, pp.201–02.

19 *Ibid.*, p.202.

20 Warburton, II, p.399.

21 *Late Proceedings of the Scots Army, op. cit.*

22 *Extract of Letters…* B.M. T.T.E.44(10).

23 *Ibid.*

24 Quoted Firth, *op. cit.*, p.204.

25 Reid, *All the King's Armies,* pp.115–16.

26 *Mercurius Aulicus*, quoted Firth, p.204.

27 Firth, p.29.

28 Firth, pp.33–34.

29 For the Yorkshire campaign see P.R. Newman, *The Defeat of John Belasyse*, in *Journal of the Yorkshire Archaeological Society*, 52, 1980, pp.50–62, and J.A. Moone, *A Brief Relation of the Life and Memoirs of John Lord Belasyse*, H.M.C Ormonde MSS, N.S. II, 1903, pp.383–85.

30 Quoted in P. Wenham, *The Great and Close Siege of York*, Kineton, 1970, p.16.

31 Reid, *All the King's Armies*, pp.118–19.

32 Wenham, *op. cit.*, pp.58–63.

Chapter 3

1   Barratt, *Cavaliers*, pp.23–26.

2   R. Hutton, *Royalist War Effort*, London, 1982, pp.130–32.

3   Barratt, *op. cit.*, p.138.

4   J. Barratt, *The Siege of Liverpool and the Lancashire Campaign 1644*, Bristol, 1993, p.5.

5   Warburton, *Memoirs*, II, pp.387–88.

6   See Chapter 2, pp.33, 38.

7   Quoted in J. Lewis (ed.), *Your Most Humble And Most Obliged Servant: Ten Secluded Letters From The Lord Byron*, Newtown, 1995, pp.5–6.

8   Barratt, *Cavaliers*, p.85.

9   *Ibid.*

10 Warburton, II, p.304.

11 British Library, *Additional MS 18981*, f.341.

12 Bodleian Library, *Carte MS* 15, f.465.

13 J. Barratt (ed.), *Prince Rupert's War: The Journal of Prince Rupert's Marches, 1642–46*, Birkenhead, 1996, pp.13–14.

14 *Carte MS*, 15, f.465.

15 *Mercurius Aulicus*, 2 June 1644, p.1008.

16 *C.S.P.D. 1644*, p.176.

17 *Ibid.*

18 *C.S.P.D., op. cit.*

19 J. Barratt, *The Siege of Liverpool*, p.8.

20 *Civil War Tracts of Lancashire*, Chetham Society, New Series, vol. 65, 1864, p.195.

21 J. Seacombe, *History of the House of Stanley*, Liverpool, 1793, p.365.

22 *Civil War Tracts*, p.195.

23 *Ibid*, Rupert *Diary*, f.33.

24 *Seacombe*, p.365.

25 *Ibid*, *Diary*, f.33; *Mercurius Aulicus*, 9 June 1644, p.1020.

26 *Seacombe*, p.365.

27 *Civil War Tracts*, p.195.

28 For the Parliamentarian version, see *Civil War Tracts*, pp.195–96; William Robinson, *Discourse of the Civil War in Lancashire*, Chetham Society, vol. 62, 1864, p.52. Royalist accounts may be found in *Diary*, f.33, *Carte MS, 10*, f.664; *15*, f.174.

29 *C.S.P.D.* 1644, pp.223–24.

30 *Ibid*, p.176.

31 Barratt, *Siege of Liverpool, op.cit.*, p.13.

32 *Carte MS, 10*, f.664.

33 *Ibid*.

34 Barratt, *Siege of Liverpool*, pp.13–14.

35 *Carte MS, 11*, f.341.

36 Quoted P. Young, *Marston Moor 1644*, Kineton, 1967, p.82.

37 Thomas Carte, *Life of James, Duke of Ormonde*, London, 1739, vol. VI, p.151.

38 Robert Byron to Ormonde, *Carte MS* 11, f.361.

39 Barratt, *Prince Rupert's War, op. cit.*, p.14.

40 *Ibid*.

41 *C.S.P.D.* 1644, pp.206–07.

42 J. Barratt, *Oswestry 1644*, in *English Civil War Times*, No. 56, p.12.

43 *C.S.P.D., op. cit.*, pp.265–66.

44 Young, *op. cit.*, p.91.

Chapter 4

1 Wenham, *Great and Close Siege of York*, pp.79–80.

2 Sir Hugh Cholmley's *Account* in *English Historical Review*, V, 189, p.347.

3 *Pythouse Papers*, p.19.

4 Cholmley, *op. cit*.

5 Firth, *Memoirs*, p.38.

6 *Diary*, quoted Young, *Marston Moor*, p.213.

7 Cholmley, *op. cit.*, p.347.

8 L. Watson's *Relation*, quoted Young, *op. cit.*,

p.228.

9 Ashe, quoted in Terry, p.267.

10 *Ibid*.

11 Watson, *op. cit*.

12 Fairfax, *Short Memorials*, quoted Young, p.242.

13 'W.H's' *Account*, quoted Young, *op. cit.*, p.247.

14 Fairfax, *op. cit.*, quoted Young, p.243.

15 Capt. Stewart's *Account*, quoted Terry, *op. cit.*, p.275.

16 *Ibid*.

17 Sir Henry Slingsby, *Diary*, quoted Young, *op. cit.*, pp.215–16.

18 Cholmley, p.348.

19 *Diary*, quoted Young, p.214.

20 Ashe, quoted Terry, p.268.

21 *Diary*, quoted Young, p.214.

22 Cholmley, p.348.

23 *Ibid*.

24 *Ibid*.

25 *Dairy*, *op.cit*.

26 Firth, *op. cit.*, pp.38–39.

27 Barratt, *Prince Rupert's War*, p.15.

28 Quoted Young, pp.86–87.

29 Quoted *ibid*.

30 P. Morrah, *Prince Rupert of the Rhine*, London, 1976, p.437, fn.43.

31 Cholmley, *op. cit*.

Chapter 5

1 The fullest examination of the terrain remains P.R. Newman, *Marston Moor, 2 July 1644: The sources and the Site*, Borthwick Papers No. 53, York 1978.

2 British Library *Add. MS 16370 f.64v–65*, reproduced in P. Young, *Marston Moor*, plate 22.

3 P. Newman, *Battle of Marston Moor*, pp.46–55.

4 J. Tincey, *Soldiers of the English Civil War (2) Cavalry*, Oxford, 1990, pp.3–4.

5 S. Reid, *Scots Armies of the English Civil War*, Oxford, 1999, p.21.

6 Tincey, pp.10–16.

7 Barratt, *Cavaliers*, p.186.

8   K. Roberts, *Soldiers of the English Civil War (1) Infantry*, Oxford, 1989, pp.13–16.

9   Barratt, *Cavaliers*, pp.35–36; Roberts, pp.22–23.

10 K. Roberts, *Battle Plans*, in *English Civil War Times*, no. 51, pp.12–15.

11 British Library *Additional MS 16370*. f.64v–65.

12 Newman, *Battle of Marston Moor*, p.91.

13 Young, pp.102–03.

14 Sir James Lumsden, *Plan of the Allied Armies at Marston Moor*, York Minster Library. Reproduced and reconstructed in Young, *op. cit.*, plate 21.

15 C. Holmes, *The Eastern Association in the English Civil War*, Cambridge, 1974, App. 8, p.238.

16 S. Reid, *All the King's Armies*, p.140 suggests as few as 8,000.

17 Watson's *Account*, printed in Young, *op. cit.*, p.229.

18 Stockdale's *Account*, in Young, pp.235–36.

19 *Ibid*.

20 Young, p.213.

21 Cholmley, p.348.

22 Quoted Firth, *Memoirs*, p.39.

23 *Ibid*, p.79.

24 Slingsby, quoted Young, p.216.

13 Ashe, quoted Terry, p.269.

14 Ashe, *op. cit.*

15 *A Full Relation*, quoted Sir Charles Firth, *Marston Moor*, in *Transactions of the Royal Historical Society*, New Series, XII, 1898, p277.

16 James II, quoted Peter Young, *Edgehill 1642*, Kineton, 1967, p.276.

17 Quoted Young, pp.247–48.

18 Newman, *Battle of Marston Moor*, p.94.

19 Stewart, quoted Terry, pp.276–77.

20 Sir Thomas Fairfax, *Short Memorials*, in Young, p.243.

21 *Ibid*.

22 Stewart, *op. cit.*

23 Monckton's *Account* in *Transactions of the Royal Historical Society*, New Series, vol. XII, 1898, pp.52–53.

24 Firth, *Memoirs*, pp.75–81.

25 *Full Relation...*, quoted Young, p.277.

26 *Sir James Lumsden's Letter to Lord Loudon*, quoted Young, p.288.

27 Ashe, quoted Terry, p.269.

28 *Full Relation*, Young, p.277.

Chapter 7

1   T. Carte, *Collection of Original Letters and Papers...*, London 1739, vol. 1, pp.55–58.

2   Cholmley, *op. cit.*, p.348.

3   *Ibid*.

4   Watson, quoted Young, *op. cit.*, p.230.

5   Denzil Lord Holles, *Memoirs*, London, 1699, p.16.

6   E. Bowles, *Manifest Truths*, 1646 (T.T.E. 343(1)).

7   Quoted Newman, *Battle of Marston Moor*, p.85.

8   Lord Saye and Sele, *Vindiciae Veritatis*, 1664 (T.T.E. 81 (13)).

9   Douglas, quoted Terry, p.281.

10 Stockdale, quoted Young, p.129.

11 Quoted Firth, *Marston Moor*, p.42 fn.

12 Stewart, quoted Terry, p.278.

13 Watson, quoted Young, p.230.

14 Ogden, quoted Young, p.217.

Chapter 6

1   Watson, *More Exact Relation...*, quoted Young, *op. cit.*, p.229.

2   Trevor, quoted Young, p.224.

3   Watson, *op. cit.*

4   Ashe, quoted Terry, *op. cit.*, p.268.

5   *Ibid*.

6   Watson, *op. cit.*

7   J. Vernon, *The Young Horseman*, London, 1644, pp.86–87.

8   Stewart, quoted Terry, p.277.

9   J.S. Clarke, *Life of James II*, London, 1816, vol. I, p.22.

10 Quoted Young, p.214.

11 Watson, quoted Young, p.230.

12 *Ibid*.

15 *Diary*, p.115.

16 *Scots Designe Discovered*, quoted Young, p.130.

17 Cholmley, p.348.

18 *Scots Designe Discovered, op. cit.*

19 Ashe, quoted Terry, p.270.

20 Fairfax, quoted Young, p.244.

21 Ogden, *op. cit.*

22 Watson, quoted Young, p.231.

23 Stockdale, quoted Young, p.236.

24 Cholmley, p.348.

25 Watson, *op. cit.*

26 Stewart, quoted Terry, p.278.

27 Watson, *op. cit.*

28 Somerville, quoted Young, p.261.

29 *Ibid.*

30 Stewart, *op. cit.*

31 Stuart Reid, *Officers and Regiments of the Royalist Armies*, Southend-on-Sea, n.d., pp.81, 91.

32 Watson, *op. cit.*

33 *Diary*, quoted Terry, p.282.

34 Monckton, quoted Young, p.222–23.

Chapter 8

1 Slingsby, *Diary*, quoted Young, *op. cit.*, p.216.

2 Ashe, quoted Terry, *op. cit.*, p.273.

3 Firth, *Memoirs*, pp.80–81.

4 Cholmley, *op. cit.*, p.350.

5 *Rupert Diary*, reprinted in Young, p.214.

6 Cholmley, p.350.

7 *Ibid.*

8 *Rupert Diary, op. cit.*

9 Earl of Clarendon, *History of the Great Rebellion*, VIII, 82.

10 Ashe, quoted Terry, p.272.

11 James, 11th Lord Somerville, *Memorie of the Somervilles*, Edinburgh 1815, Vol. II, pp.343–52.

12 Ashe, quoted Terry, p.273.

13 Ogden's *Account*, in Young, pp.217–18.

14 *Mercurius Aulicus*, 6 July 1644, p.1072.

15 Slingsby, p.114.

16 *Ibid.*

17 Newman, *Battle of Marston Moor*, p.135.

18 *Discourse, op. cit.*, pp.54–55.

19 British Library, *Additional MS 18981*, f.227–28.

20 *Ibid.*

21 Clarendon, VIII, p.141.

22 Byron, *op cit.*

BIBLIOGRAPHY

Primary Sources

Ashe, S., *A Continuation of True Intelligence*, July 1644
(reprinted in C.S Terry, *Life of Alexander Leslie*).

Barratt, J. (ed.), *Prince Rupert's War: the Journal of
Prince Rupert's Marches*, Birkenhead, 1996.

Beaumont, W. (ed.), *A Discourse of the Warr in
Lancashire*, Chetham Society, Old Series, Vol. lxii,
Manchester 1864.

Bodleian Library, *Carte MS, 11, 15*.

Bowles, E., *Manifest Truths*, London, 1646, British
Library *T.T.E. 34(39)*.

Calendar of State Papers Domestic, 1644.

British Library, *Additional MS 18981* (Prince Rupert
Correspondence).

Carte, T., *Collection of Original Letters and Papers*, Vol.
1, London 1739.

Cholmley, Sir Hugh, *Memorials Touching the Battle of
York*, in *English Historical Review*.

Clarendon, Earl of, *History of the Great Rebellion*,
Oxford, 1880.

De Gomme, Sir Bernard, *Order of His Majestie's Armie*,
British Library *Add. MS 16370, f.64.* (reproduced
in Young, *Marston Moor*, plate 22).

Douglas, R., *Diary* (reprinted in Terry, *Life of
Alexander Leslie*, pp.280–83).

Fairfax, Sir Thomas, *Short Memorials* (reprinted in
Young, *Marston Moor*, pp.240–45).

Firth, C.H. (ed.), *Memoirs of William Cavendish, Duke
of Newcastle*, London, 1906.

Fuller, T., *Worthies of England*, London, 1811.

Holles, D., *Memoirs*, London, 1699.

Hopton, Lord Ralph, *Bellum Civile*, Taunton, 1902.

Laing, D. (ed.), *Letters and Journals of Robert Baillie*,
Edinburgh, 1842.

Late Proceedings of the Scots Armie, 1644, British
Library, *T.T.E. 2(31)*.

Lewis, J. (ed.), *Your Most Humble and Most Obliged
Servant: Ten Secluded Letters from the Lord Byron*,
Newtown, 1995.

Lilly, W., *History of His Life and Times*, London, 1826.

Lumsden, Sir James, *Letter to Lord Loudon* (reprinted
in Young, *Marston Moor*, pp.267–69).

Lumsden, Sir James, *Plan of the Allied Armies at
Marston Moor* (York Minster Library) (reproduced
with additions in Young, *Marston Moor*, plate 21).

Mercurius Aulicus, Oxford 1644.

Monckton, Sir Philip, *Memoir* (reprinted in Young,
Marston Moor, pp.222–23).

Moone, J., *A Brief Relation of the Life and Memoirs of
John Lord Belasyse*, H.M.C. *Ormonde MSS*, New
Series, II, London, 1903.

Ormerod, G. (ed.), *Tracts Relating to Military Proceedings
in Lancashire During The Great Civil War*, Chetham
Society, Old Series, Vol. ii, Manchester, 1844.

Rupert Diary, Wiltshire County Record Office
(reprinted in Young, *Marston Moor*, pp.212–13).

Somerville, Lord James, *Memorie of the Somervilles*,
Edinburgh, 1815.

Stewart, Capt. W., *A Full Account of the Victory
Obtained…* British Library T.T.E. 54(19) (reprinted
in Terry, *Life of Alexander Leslie*, pp.274–80).

Stockdale, T., *Letter to John Rushworth*, British
Library, *Harleian MS 166, f.87* (reprinted in
Young, *Marston Moor*, pp.234–38).

Turner, Sir James, *Memoirs of his Life and Times*,

Edinburgh, 1839.

Vicars, J., *Parliamentary Chronicles*, London, 1646.

'W.H.' *A Relation of the Good Successe...* British Library T.T.E. 54(11) (reprinted in Young, *Marston Moor*, pp.246–49).

Warwick, Sir Philip, *Memoires of the Reign of King Charles the First*, London, 1701.

Watson, L., *A More Exact Relation of the late Battell neare York*, British Library, T.T.E. 2(14) (reprinted in Yong, *Marston Moor*, pp.227–32).

Secondary Sources

Appleby, D., *Our Fall Our Fame*, Newtown, 1996.

Barratt, J., *Battle of Nantwich, 1644*, Bristol, 1993.

Barratt, J., *Cavaliers: The Royalist Army at War, 1642–46*, Stroud, 2000.

Barratt, J., *'Cure for the Scots': Troops from Ireland and the Royalist War Effort*, in *English Civil War Times*, nos 54–56.

Barratt, J., *Oswestry 1644*, in *English Civil War Times*, no. 56, pp.13–16.

Barratt, J., *The Siege of Liverpool and the Lancashire Campaign, 1644*, Bristol, 1993.

Burne, A.H., *The Battlefields of England*, London, 1950.

Clark, J. (ed.), *Life of James II*, London, 1816.

Day, W.A. (ed.) *The Pythouse Papers*, London, 1879.

Firth, C.H., *Marston Moor*, in *Transactions of the Royal Historical Society*, New Series, Vol. xii, 1898.

Furgol, E.M., *Regimental History of the Covenanting Armies*, Edinburgh, 1990.

Gardiner, S.R., *History of the Great Civil War*, London, 1904.

Gilbert, J.K., *History of the Irish Confederacy*, Dublin, 1879.

Holmes, C., *The Eastern Association in the English Civil War*, Cambridge, 1974.

Hutton, R., *The Royalist War Effort*, London, 1982.

Ives, E.W., *Drums Along the Weaver*, in *Cheshire Round*, 1963.

Lowe, J., *Campaign of the Irish-Royalist Army in Cheshire*, in *Transactions of the Historic Society of Lancashire and Cheshire*, Vol. 111, 1959.

Malcolm, J.L., *'All the King's Men': The Impact of the Crown's Irish Soldiers in the English Civil War*, in *Irish Historical Studies*, Vol. xxi, no. 83, 1979.

Morrah, P., *Prince Rupert of the Rhine*, London, 1976.

Newman, P., *The Battle of Marston Moor, 1644*, Chichester, 1981.

Newman, P., *The Defeat of Lord Belasyse*, in *Journal of the Yorkshire Archaeological Society*, 52, 1980, pp.13–28.

Newman, P., *The Old Service*, Manchester, 1993.

Newman, P.R., *Marston Moor, 2 July 1644: The Sources and the Site*, Borthwick Papers, no. 53, York, 1978.

Reid, S., *All the King's Armies: A Military History of the Civil Wars*, Staplehurst, 1998.

Reid, S., *Officers and Regiments of the Royalist Army*, Southend-on-Sea, n.d.

Reid, S., *Scots Armies of the English Civil War*, Oxford, 1999.

Reid, S., *Scots Armies of the Seventeenth Century I*, Southend-on-Sea, 1989.

Roberts, K., *Soldiers of the English Civil War (1) Infantry*, Oxford 1989.

Roberts, K., *Battle Plans*, in *English Civil War Times*, no. 51, pp.12–15.

Ryder, I., *An English Army for Ireland*, Southend-on-Sea, 1989.

Seacombe, J., *History of the House of Stanley*, Liverpool, 1793.

Tincey, J., *Soldiers of the English Civil War (2) Cavalry*, Oxford, 1990.

Terry, C.S. *Life and Campaigns of Alexander Leslie, Earl of Leven*, Glasgow, 1899.

Terry, C.S., *The Scottish Campaign in Northumberland and Durham*, in *Archaelogia Aeliana*, New Series, Vol. xxi, 1899.

Warburton, E., *Memoirs of Prince Rupert and the Cavaliers*, 3 vols, London, 1849.

Wedgewood, C.V., *The King's War*, London, 1957.

Wenham, P., *The Great and Close Siege of York*, Kineton, 1970.

Woolrych, A., *Battles of the English Civil War*, London, 1961.

Young, P., *Marston Moor 1644*, Kineton, 1970.

LIST OF ILLUSTRATIONS

Unless otherwise stated, all illustrations are from the collection of the author.
PP – Partizan Press

Colour Plates

The Battlefield

INDEX

Page numbers in *italic* refer to illustrations

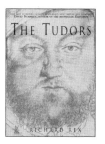
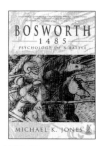